The Grail Mystery
and the Seven Liberal Arts

Frans Lutters

**The Grail Mystery
and the Seven Liberal Arts**

Translated by Philip Mees

Waldorf
PUBLICATIONS

Published by:

Waldorf Publications at the
Research Institute for Waldorf Education
38 Main Street
Chatham, New York 12037

Title: *The Grail Mystery and the Seven Liberal Arts*
Author: Frans Lutters
Translation: Philip Mees
Layout/design: Ann Erwin
Proofreading: Colleen Shetland
ISBN #978-1-936367-65-8

Originally published in Dutch as
Het Graalmysterie en de Zeven Vrije Kunsten
by Nearchus C.V., Assen, Netherlands, 2006
Printed by Zijlstra Drukwerk, Rijswijk
Copyright Frans Lutters, Driebergen 2006
ISBN 90-73310-44-X

Cover: Sandro Botticelli, *Youth Introduced into the
Circle of Wisdom and the Liberal Arts*
Back cover: Piero del Pollaiolo, *Temperance* (upper left) and
Fortitude (lower right), two of the Seven Virtues

Alanus ab Insulis (left) as troubadour

Dedicated
to the Waldorf school movement
in the English-speaking world
and to my beloved wife and sons,
in the good spirit of Phronesis.

Table of Contents

Part 3 – Insight into the Mystery

Foreword

This book has come into being as a result of my lectures and workshops in the course of more than 25 years on the renewal of the Seven Liberal Arts and the Mystery of the Grail. For me, these two different subjects, the Grail and the liberal arts, gradually grew together into a joint spiritual path of practice and experience. For a long time the book remained a workbook that circulated among workshop participants; only much later has it grown into a real book.

This way of working is consistent with the spirit in which things were done in the famous medieval School of Chartres in France, the Cathedral school that attracted students from every corner of Europe and even from the Arab world. Its teaching methodology revolved around the dialogue between teacher and student, and equally important was the search for connecting links between art and science. Subjects such as grammar, astronomy, mathematics, and so forth, were not taught for their own sake, but were put in service of the moral development of the human being.

In collaboration and dialogue with workshop participants, on trips to Chartres with groups, and also in my work as a Waldorf high school teacher, again and again I came to new insights and experiences, of which the book you are now holding in your hands is the result. The spirit of Chartres seemed to embrace my work and always brought me new questions and insights. The book is both a study that opens new perspectives to the readers and also a guide to exercises they can do on their own.

The book thus received its beginning in Chartres, the place where, in the Middle Ages, the teaching of the Seven Liberal Arts was given out of direct inspiration of the Grail. The story of Parzival's search for the Grail is the source of this inspiration, and it is also an example of a new way of learning and teaching.

As a Waldorf school teacher I have many times had the privilege of working through the story about the Quest for the Grail with 17-year-olds. Every time it was brought home to me that this is no antiquated story but is all about today's youth. My 30 years of experience as a teacher at several Waldorf schools is to me a source of confidence in the inspiration and creativity of the young people of today.

Therefore, this book is dedicated most of all to them. But I also hope to be able to inspire parents, grandparents and teachers to go and explore new forms of learning and experience, so that they can accompany young people on their authentic and often very individual paths. May this book lead readers to new ideas and to new spiritual perspectives of their own research and explorations into learning processes and moral development.

The liberal arts are actually well-known in the Anglo-Saxon world with its liberal arts colleges where students are offered a broad program of study and research. Nowhere else have I experienced more harmony between my personal strivings and those of the cultural and scientific communities in general. It is therefore a source of satisfaction to me to see that this book has now become accessible to the English-speaking world.

I want to express my gratitude to all those who have helped make this book possible. Dick Blokker organized many courses in Holland on the renewal of the liberal arts, as well as study trips to Chartres. Philip Mees translated my original Dutch text into English, and Patrice Maynard, Director of Publications and Development at the Research Institute for Waldorf Education, has made the publication of the English edition possible. And last but not least, my dear wife Ineke was and is my companion and supporter on trips and workweeks in Chartres, while my sons never cease to give me inspiration toward new discoveries of the tremendous new capacities living in abundance in the youth of our time.

Frans Lutters
Driebergen, Netherlands
September 2014

Introduction

The Seven Liberal Arts formed the foundation of European education in the Middle Ages. The seven arts—Grammatica, Rhetorica, Dialectica, Arithmetica, Geometria, Musica and Astronomia—were called "free" because, while the scientific content of each art was well-defined, the teacher developed his own approach to the form in which he presented it. The liberal arts were also free because they were, to a certain extent, free from interference by the Church.

The Seven Liberal Arts were taught in two parts: the Trivium and the Quadrivium. The curriculum began with the Trivium which consisted of Grammatica, Rhetorica and Dialectica. After completion of the Trivium, the student usually had to travel to a larger city to follow the Quadrivium, which was oriented toward measure, number and space: Arithmetica, Geometria, Musica and Astronomia. When the student had mastered all seven arts, he could become a Master in the Liberal Arts.

What was not realized by many was that this curriculum in seven steps was also a path of initiation that had a direct connection with the mystery of the Holy Grail. I will describe this path here as an adventure that has spiritual value also for our time.

Besides his own studies, a medieval Master in the Liberal Arts drew from an important source: the book *De Nuptiis Philologiae et Mercurii* (The Marriage of Philologia and Mercury), written by Martianus Capella in the fifth century CE. This was the most important standard work on the liberal arts and was used by practically all subsequent authors as the basis of their own reflections and observations.

Martianus Capella was a contemporary of St. Augustine (354–430) and, like him, was born in North Africa. At that time the teaching of Mani (Manichaeism) was widely spread, also in North Africa. Mani had searched for a Christian path of initiation that would be compatible with the pre-Christian mysteries, and for this reason he was fervently opposed by St. Augustine. Martianus Capella certainly knew all these views. His book shows deep spiritual knowledge. He described the Seven Liberal Arts as seven virgins. These are the ones who teach the liberal arts. We thus read that the Seven Liberal Arts were still experienced as direct inspirations from seven heavenly virgins. Martianus Capella was the first one to describe them in concrete detail.

About 700 years later, a famous teacher in Chartres, Alanus ab Insulis (Alain de Lille, 1128–1203), was one of the last to describe these seven virgins in vivid liveliness. Alanus ab Insulis is a personality shrouded in riddles. But he brings us closer to the mystery of the Grail.

PART 1
SEVEN SOURCES OF INSPIRATION

1 The Sevenfold Way

The number seven in ancient cultures

Although much was written about the liberal arts in the Middle Ages, their origin goes back to pre-Christian times. All ancient cultures attached great importance to seven as the number in which wisdom is revealed.

The culture of *ancient India* looked for its origin in the seven Rishis. The Vedas tell that they were pupils of Manu, who was the first to give the people moral laws. These Rishis appeared to be very simple people, but when the seven of them were united, they revealed great wisdom that encompassed the entire cosmos. As in other cultures, in Indian thinking the moon marks the last phase the human soul goes through before it is born on earth. Wisdom-filled beings, who work together with the angels, dwell in the moon sphere. In Indian philosophy these wisdom-filled beings were called Pitris. The seven Rishis taught out of the inspiration they received from the Pitris. According to Rudolf Steiner, the Pitris are the "primeval teachers of humanity."

Long ago the Pitris withdrew from the earth, and since then they have had their supersensible dwelling place within the "stronghold of the moon." Here they observe the courses of the planets. And in this ever-moving weaving of the planets, they read the destiny of the human individuality who entered the moon sphere on the way to the approaching moment of its next earthly birth. The primeval teachers of humanity exert a formative influence on the life forces of the becoming human being.

Out of the qualities of the planets, the primeval teachers work on the destiny of the human individuality. Thus they accompany the destiny of the human being, which arose on the basis of past lives, in the new life. One could call them the "guardians of the diary" of the human being on the way from one life to another. The Bhagavad Gita was written out of this knowledge.

In the original *Iranian or Persian* culture, Zarathustra spoke of the seven good spirits who serve the Sun Spirit, Ahura Mazdao. They are called the seven Amshaspands. They bring the good to humanity in deeds, words and thought. According to Greek tradition, Zarathustra was the first spiritual teacher of the Iranian culture, about 5000 to 6000 years before the Christian era. About 500 to 600 years BCE, Zoroaster renewed the teaching of Zarathustra and spoke of the battle between light and dark, good and evil. He taught of seven light beings around the "Great Sun Aura," Ahura Mazdao, and five Devas, dark beings around Angra Mainyu, Ahriman.[1]

In the *Jewish* culture we know the seven-branched candelabra, the Menorah, in memory of the seven days of creation by the Elohim. From time immemorial humanity knew that the creation was built on the principle of seven. Seven is still preserved in the seven days of the week, and the first seven phases of Creation are described in the book Genesis in the Old Testament. The Torah is based on seven.

Genesis, the sacred book of Jewish culture, begins with the words:

B'reishit bara Elohim et hashamayim ve'et ha'aretz.

Genesis here mentions not one God, Eloha, but seven Elohim. In the Menorah we find not only an expression of the seven days of creation, but also a picture of the sevenfold human being who was created in the image and likeness of the Elohim.

Rudolf Steiner (1861–1925), the founder of anthroposophy, pointed to a very early description of the virgins of the Seven Liberal Arts in the Old Testament. He meant the moment when Moses, in his flight from Egypt, encountered the seven daughters of Jethro at a spring in the desert, where they wanted to fill their water jugs and where he protected them from shepherds who were threatening them.

The account of the experiences of Moses while he was a disciple of this great, wise priest [Jethro] opens with a description of his meeting with Jethro's seven daughters [in the land of Midian, Exodus 2:15,16] near a well (a symbol betokening a source of wisdom). Anyone who would comprehend the deeper significance underlying a graphic narrative of this nature must remember above all that mystical descriptions of every period have symbolically portrayed all such knowledge and power as the soul itself may display in the form of female figures—even down to Goethe, who in the closing words of *Faust* alludes to the "eternal feminine." In the seven daughters of Jethro, then, we recognize the seven human soul forces over which that priestly character exercised control.[2]

During the *Egyptian* culture Thoth-Hermes brought a sevenfold wisdom. In the *Corpus Hermeticum* he speaks about seven as follows:

> And Heaven was seen in seven circles; its Gods were visible in forms of stars with all their signs; while Nature had her members made articulate together with the Gods in her.[3]

A legendary manuscript, a report of an Egyptian initiation that, according to tradition, originated with the Greek philosopher Iamblichus, gives a picture of seven in relation to the goddess Isis:

> ... the Goddess Isis ... the Great Mother ...
> This image is composed of equal parts:
> Lead, the metal consecrated to Remtha – the Heavenly Bull (Saturn)
> Tin, the metal consecrated to Pi-Zeous – the Traveling Star (Jupiter)
> Iron, the metal consecrated to Ertosie – the Red Horus (Mars)
> Gold, the metal consecrated to Pi-Ra – the Heavenly Sun (Sun)
> Copper, the metal consecrated to Suroth – the Morning Star (Venus)
> Mercury, the metal consecrated to Thoth-Hermes – the Heavenly
>   Messenger (Mercury)
> Silver, the metal consecrated to Pi-Loh – the Silver Moon (Moon).

On her head, Isis wears a triangular silver diadem and within its center is a motif with twelve rays; on her breast she wears a gold cross and within its center is a red rosette as symbol of all that was revealed. The cross represents both infinity and the soul as it manifests itself in the material world. Isis stretches her hands slightly in front of her body and thus forms a triangle, with the head as the crown while the open hands with the fingers spread send golden rays to the earth.[4]

It is noteworthy that Isis is here described in relation to the seven metals of the planets. She also wears a triangle on her forehead and a cross that forms a square on her breast.

Education in the Middle Ages

This picture corresponds with the symbols that were used in the Middle Ages to indicate the subjects of the Trivium and the Quadrivium. The triangle encompasses the realm of the word, the Logos, the creative Word—grammar, rhetoric and dialectic—in which the wisdom of the soul reveals itself. The square indicates the world in which wisdom expresses itself in the form of the laws of numbers—arithmetic, geometry, music and astronomy. Together, triangle and square reveal the sevenfold nature of creation. In the Middle Ages, Mary was depicted in the West Portal of Chartres Cathedral as Queen of Heaven surrounded by the Seven Liberal Arts. There she is shown as *Mary-Sophia*.*

The Virgin Mary-Sophia stands with the moon under her feet; she is victorious, but out of the powers of the sun and stars she also protects the becoming child. Besides the sphere of influence of the moon, the Virgin Mary-Sophia also encompasses the sun and the stars. She is clothed with the sun and crowned with twelve stars.[5] In ancient Egypt, Isis was also always shown with the moon.

The founder of the School of Chartres, Fulbertus (952–1028), was deeply conscious of the Virgin Sophia. He called her Mary, the Star of the Sea (*Stella Maris*), and described her significance for education in the Seven Liberal Arts. He wrote many poems dedicated to her.

The School of Chartres was famous in the 11th and 12th centuries for its teachers such as Bernardus Silvestris and Alanus ab Insulis, who taught the Seven Liberal Arts in eminent ways. Egyptian Isis wisdom was brought to new life here within Christianity.

---

* *Sophia* is the Greek word for *wisdom*. (P.M.)

In Martianus Capella's book, which was of such fundamental significance for the Seven Liberal Arts and was also used in Chartres, the virgin who teaches the first of the liberal arts, grammar, says that she came from Egypt, and that only later she connected herself with Greek and subsequently also with Latin culture. She places her essential being in the culture of ancient Egypt. The other virgins make similar note of the connections they have with ancient Egypt.[6]

The path of learning through the Seven Liberal Arts was described by the famous Irish philosopher John Scotus Eriugena (810–877), who was the leader of the palace school of Charles the Bald. In his book *De Divisione Naturae* he introduced the division between Trivium and Quadrivium in the Seven Liberal Arts. The study of the Seven Liberal Arts in their entirety leads through Philo-Sophia (love of wisdom) to the possibility of a direct experience of the Trinity.

Charlemagne and education in the liberal arts

Around the year 800 Charlemagne laid the foundation for a new educational system in Europe. In the footsteps of his predecessors his counselor, Alcuin, divided the curriculum into seven parts, the liberal arts. In this way, the Anglo-Saxon Alcuin renewed the path of learning and exercise in seven steps that formed the basis of education in Europe in the Middle Ages.

For Alcuin, who founded the court school of Charlemagne, the curriculum through the Seven Liberal Arts was of particular educational value, both for youths who would in future have a spiritual task and for those who were destined for a worldly task. The principal aim of the study of the Seven Liberal Arts was to acquire virtuous wisdom through the discipline of a stepwise and strict practice of science. Alcuin described the purpose of education in the Seven Liberal Arts in his book *Disputatio de Vera Philosophia* (*Treatise on True Philosophy*) as follows:

Solomon said that Wisdom (Sophia) built a house resting on seven pillars. This sentence can be applied to Christ Himself, who built his physical entity in the body of Mary and in doing so was supported by the seven gifts of the Holy Spirit. This saying can refer to the school itself, as the House of God, endowed by divine wisdom with the seven gifts. In every condition of life, Wisdom rests on the seven pillars of the liberal arts.

In learning one can only attain complete science when one raises himself in seven steps, or along seven pillars, to wisdom. Everyone is able to tread this path of the seven steps of philosophy. But divine mercy is a condition for this path and, as teacher, even necessary.

For Alcuin, as for so many others, the most important book on the Seven Liberal Arts was *The Marriage of Philologia and Mercury* by Martianus Capella, who described the connection of human consciousness, expressed in the being of Philologia, with Mercury, the messenger of the gods who connected heaven and earth. During the wedding the Seven Liberal Arts appear as female figures who all bestow their powers on Philologia, the representative of the learning human soul, so that she may become virtuous and can be filled with cosmic wisdom.

In the traditions in which, from time immemorial, the seven aspects of the human soul were recognized, the female figures who guard the liberal arts are the mediators between cosmic star wisdom and the human soul.

The mirror of Till Eulenspiegel

Till Eulenspiegel is a renowned figure in European history. With his jests and antics he held up a mirror to people. Just like Parzival he was a kind of "pure fool."

The moon stands in the firmament like a mirror for the sunlight. In its changing phases it sometimes forms a sickle; at Easter time it is even a sickle on its back, like a vessel. It is as if at the time of the death and resurrection of Christ the Grail appears in the heavens as a sign.

In 1867, Charles de Coster[7] described Till Eulenspiegel as a human being who goes through a path of initiation. He experiences death and resurrection, an initiation that can be viewed as a modern Grail initiation. In his novel, Charles de Coster goes so far as to make the destiny of the Netherlands dependent on the question of whether the human being, represented in the novel by Till Eulenspiegel, is able to complete this path successfully. Till Eulenspiegel's path is a path of initiation based on the Seven Liberal Arts.

Many old initiations took place in seven stages. Among the Romans, for instance, the Mithras initiation was very popular. This initiation went back to Zoroaster who lived in Babylon at the time of King Cyrus the Great and the Babylonian captivity of the Jews in the sixth century BCE. The prophet Daniel and the Greek philosopher Pythagoras both met this initiate in Babylon. His teaching was handed down in the *Zend Avesta*.

The stages of the Mithras mysteries carry different names. In the first stage the candidate was called a raven; in the succeeding stages he was called successively the occult one, warrior, lion, folk spirit, sun hero and father. In these seven stages the candidate also became acquainted with the forces of the entire planetary system as these can be perceived in the visible planets Mercury, Venus, Mars, Jupiter, Saturn, Sun and Moon.

At the end of Charles de Coster's novel, Till Eulenspiegel goes through an arduous trial and speaks the following words: "The ashes beat on my heart. Would that Christ could manifest those Seven whose ashes, scattered by the wind, would make Flanders and the whole world happy."

Sirius, the star of Zarathustra and Isis

Till Eulenspiegel then points to heaven. "Perhaps if a spirit will descend from the cold star," says Eulenspiegel pointing to Sirius with his finger. Sirius was traditionally the star that was consecrated to Isis for the Egyptians and to Zarathustra for the Iranians. This is the star Eulenspiegel points to, while he calls upon Christ to demonstrate the power of seven. Zarathustra taught that there are seven good planetary spirits that, through the power of the sun, can bring about the resurrection of the earth.

The story continues. Till and his beloved Nele are thrown to the ground by a force of nature: "And indeed, Eulenspiegel and Nele saw in the grass, in the sky and in heaven seven luminous copper tablets secured by seven flaming nails. On the tablets were the words:

Under the dung heap sprouts the plant
Is seven bad, is seven good.
Coal does form the diamond,
The foolish doctor, the wise apprentice.
Is seven bad, is seven good."

Then they see seven vices that are thrown into the fire in order to rise from the ashes again, but now as seven virtues. With joy and confidence in the future, the tried and tested soul of Till now hears the following:

When over land and waters
These seven, transformed, shall reign,
People, look high!
The world is saved!

The human soul is addressed in its virtue. In Egypt it was the veiled goddess Isis who accompanied the sevenfold development of the human soul. Her star is the one which Till and Nele saw in its brilliance: It is Sirius!

Charles de Coster shows us that he is conscious of an ever-progressing stream in the spiritual history of humanity. That which had its origin with Zoroaster, is continued in our time. The trials of initiation are transformed into virtues and are, in a mysterious way, connected with Christ. Mysteriously we hear the words: "Would that Christ could manifest those Seven!"

These words form a connection with the goals of the education in the liberal arts of the Middle Ages. In its sevenfold form, the education that was built up in seven stages was a continuation of the path of the ancient mysteries.

The way of Parzival to the Grail

Just like Till Eulenspiegel, Parzival begins his search for the Grail as an open-minded pupil who knows nothing but wants to learn everything. Wolfram von Eschenbach describes Parzival as a seeker. After many trials and wanderings he is, in the end, called to the Grail. There sound the names of the seven moving stars. It is Kundry, the messenger of the Grail, who speaks the names of these seven heavenly bodies, but she does so in a remarkable way, namely by using their Arabic names:

> Mark now, Parzival:
> The highest of the planets, Zval,
> And the swiftly moving Almustri,
> Almaret and the bright Samsi [Sun],
> All show good fortune for you here.
> The fifth is named Alligafir.
> Under these the sixth is Alkiter,
> And nearest us is Alkamer [Moon].[8]

Shortly before this passage mentioning the seven planets, Wolfram speaks of the great Greek initiate Pythagoras. Here hides a reference to the path of schooling of the Middle Ages through the practice of the Seven Liberal Arts.

> ... the wise Pictagoras, who was an astronomer and without doubt so wise that no one since Adam's time can be compared to him ...

Of the Greeks it was Pythagoras who described the Seven Liberal Arts and especially the Quadrivium which he called *ta mathema*. It is known that Pythagoras lived for many years in Egypt and absorbed there the wisdom of the Egyptians. He was also a pupil of Zoroaster in Babylon, the great initiated teacher who renewed the wisdom of Zarathustra. Pythagoras applied himself particularly to music as the all-encompassing science within the Quadrivium. On the West Portal of the cathedral in Chartres he is therefore shown as the teacher who practiced music.

Trithem von Sponheim and the intelligences of the planets

This awareness of the sevenfold nature of the human soul remained preserved into later times. During the Renaissance, Trithem von Sponheim (1462–1516) wrote a book on the seven intelligences of the planets.

Out of a Christian tradition he described seven divine beings that were called archangels by St. Paul and his friend Dionysius the Areopagite. He connected these seven archangels with the seven planets as follows:

Gabriel	–	Moon
Raphael	–	Mercury
Anael	–	Venus
Michael	–	Sun
Samael	–	Mars
Zachariel	–	Jupiter
Oriphiel	–	Saturn

In the Middle Ages, angels and archangels were sometimes called intelligences. According to Basil Valentine (Basilius Valentinus, 15th century), the practice of the Seven Liberal Arts has to do with the development of intelligence, but also with the development of the seven virtues.

Basil Valentine and the Seven Liberal Arts

Both Trithem and his older contemporary Basil Valentine were abbots of monasteries. Basil made an unqualified connection between the Seven Liberal Arts, the intelligences of the planets and the seven virtues. Working with the liberal arts, he said, makes a human being virtuous in a sevenfold way. His insights are a fruitful foundation for working with the Seven Liberal Arts and are therefore the basis for this book. Basil Valentine is the name of a mysterious alchemist who lived in the 15th century. Several of his works have been preserved; one of these is a treatise on the Seven Liberal Arts which he wrote in the form of a poem.[9] Here follow excerpts relating to the seven planetary intelligences:

Michael is the intelligence of the Sun. Sunday is his day.
    The key to the great secret
    Gives *Michael*, that angel mine.
    Grammatica is my Liberal Art.
    Read in the book and find my gift.

Then you can speak truth,
For *Justitia* is still alive.
My son wears the carbuncle stone
And is therefore to no one akin.
Because I consult high guides
Sunday is my day and hour.

Gabriel is the intelligence of the Moon. Monday is his day.
Set in gold was the sapphire,
Translucent blue in color and radiance
The best art is what I know:
Dialectica is who I am.
I speak as a virgin ought:
Prudentia lives in every word.
My body, soul and spirit
Were always with my king.
Monday is my dedicated day,
On this day I am joyful.

Samael is the intelligence of Mars. Tuesday is his day.
Samael is my angel good.
Should he not have guarded me,
I would have tasted death
And lived my life in the underworld.
My sword is of pure steel
But the ruby speaks the same language.
Peace is not my goal,
Fortitudo feels good to me.
On *Tuesday* I have power
Unexpected by some.

Raphael is the intelligence of Mercury. Wednesday is his day.
Wednesday is my choice,
On that day I was born.

All the colors of the earth
Were by my mother kept for me.
Therefore *Raphael* bestowed a crystal on me
From which I shall fashion all.
Raphael gave me the power
That brought me back to *Mercury*.
I then also received my task
Which makes *Arithmetica* my pupil.
And now pay attention to my face:
Mere mercury gives me no weight.

Zachariel is the intelligence of Jupiter. Thursday is his day.
Long ago I was teacher to many,
Reason why I am as a god revered,
And especially on *Thursday*
My virtues were plain to all.
This is still my day.
My angel's name is *Zachariel*.
Rhetorica moves my tongue
And the topaz bestows power on me.
Because I practice without ceasing
Hope shall never abandon me.

Anael is the intelligence of Venus. Friday is his day.
Musica is my Liberal Art,
I reign with it the life of love.
The sound of strings shows who I was,
Therefore my virtue is *Charitas*.
Anael is my eminent angel,
He preserves me from ill-luck and trick.
He also bestowed on me a precious stone,
The emerald shining vivid green.
And then I greet a blessed night;
Friday is the day I gladly await.

Oriphiel is the intelligence of Saturn. Saturday is his day.

I am descended from highest heaven,
Saturday is the day that receives my power.
A garnet brilliantly shining
Gave me the angel *Oriphiel.*
Astronomia is my Liberal Art.
Common lead I favor not.

It is striking that Basil places Rhetoric with Zachariel and does not mention the Liberal Art belonging to Samael. As we will see, there is much to be said for the idea that Rhetoric also falls under Samael, and that Geometry is also inspired by Zachariel.

In search of a sevenfold image of the human being

From this introductory picture it will have become clear that the practice of the Seven Liberal Arts is not an isolated path but has deep relationships with many cultures. The mysterious alchemists and Rosicrucians have also preserved their relationship to the number seven. They are still as timely as ever. In the early 20th century it was Rudolf Steiner who demonstrated the connection of seven with the principle of development and, on this basis, pointed the way toward a renewed practice of the Seven Liberal Arts. In his book *Theosophy,*[10] he gave a seven-membered picture of the human being. In anthroposophy this view is made accessible again to modern thinking by the following description of the seven elements of the human being:

> The *physical body* is immediately perceptible to the senses. It is easily noticed that it consists of three principal parts: head, trunk and limbs.
>
> It is more difficult to perceive and understand the *formative forces* or the *etheric body*. It is a closed system of organic forces that look after and operate the physical body, and stream through it as life processes.
>
> The *soul* is carried by the *astral body* and can be observed by a clairvoyant as the aura with its play of multiple colors. It is built up out of the seven aspects of the planets.

The "I" manifests itself in a completely individual manner and is connected with the eternal biography of the human being from life to life through the periods of review and preparation in between. In future the "I" is to transform the first three elements and develop out of them three additional, spiritual elements:

The transformed and purified astral body forms the *spirit self*, in Indian philosophy called *Manas*.

The transformed etheric body, which is also the seat of our habits, forms the basis of *life spirit*, called *Buddhi* in Indian thought.

And the fully transformed physical body becomes point of departure for *spirit man*, *Atman,* in Indian philosophy.

The structure and sequence of the Seven Liberal Arts, as taught in antiquity and the Middle Ages, also work in this image of the human being that Rudolf Steiner developed anew for our time. Because the full sevenfoldness of the human being still lies in the future, and demands a great deal of effort on the part of the individual person, working with the Seven Liberal Arts as such is not out of date. But this effort does ask for new methods that are appropriate for our age, now that learning has become more and more an individual matter.

Now, in the early 21st century, we are more than ever aware of the fact that the creation is as yet unfinished. This unfinished creation calls for the creativity and moral responsibility of human beings themselves. There are no longer any gods who can carry us, and no laws that can fully protect us. The environment tells us that there are limits to growth and that life is asking for protection and appropriate management.

We shall only be able to give answers to all these questions if we are capable of placing ourselves in a new, individual and free manner in the stream of creative principles. Then it will become evident how fruitful a sevenfold image of the human being can be for a modern, spiritual consciousness which has as its goal not to remain on the fringes of world development but, where possible, to take responsibility for the future of the earth and humanity.

2 The Journey Begins

In 1922, Walter Johannes Stein was asked by Rudolf Steiner to teach literature in the 11th grade of the first Waldorf school. In reply to his question as to which epic he should choose for the period of the Middle Ages, Rudolf Steiner asked him to make his own suggestion. Walter Johannes Stein then proposed *Parzival* in the version of Wolfram von Eschenbach.[11]

That was the beginning of Stein's lifelong search for the mystery of the Grail in which also the Seven Liberal Arts were to play an important role. In subsequent years he taught the adventures and vicissitudes of Parzival again and again. In the process, he developed an increasing ability to put himself in the shoes of the hermit Trevrezent, Parzival's teacher. Six years later he wrote a book about his experiences including conversations between Trevrezent and Parzival.[12]

Stein described the relationship between the Seven Liberal Arts and the mystery of the Grail in a lecture he gave on June 25, 1932, in Glastonbury, England.[13] In this lecture, Stein gave an extensive report of a conversation between the Grail seeker Trevrezent and the knight Schionatulander. He had not yet been able to write about this in his earlier book (1928). The remarkable part of this description is that Stein seems to be speaking of something he had experienced himself.

In this conversation the path of learning through the Seven Liberal Arts becomes visible, and Stein brings it into relation with the mystery of the Grail. An archetypal picture opened itself to him of a joint learning process in the collaboration between teacher and pupil.

The Seven Liberal Arts are vividly called to life *in their active, living powers*. Because the conversation sheds so much light on the Seven Liberal Arts, I have quoted important parts of the lecture below.

One day a youth [Schionatulander] came to the old man [Trevrezent] to take rest on a long journey. The youth asked many questions to which the old man responded.

28

The old man said: "Look, the grass grows and the flowers in the grass are blossoming. But you overlook many things if you stop there and seek no further explanation of what you see. If you want to understand reality you have to learn to see through the appearances which provide such a spectacle for the eyes. Something makes the grass grow.

"To discover what it is, you have to pass from the observation of external appearances to interior listening. If you pay close attention, you will recognize that the act of remembering an observation is a listening process. A wonderful musicality in things will one day be revealed to you if you live with this thought and repeatedly pass from observation to inner listening. The whole of the plant world will resound. The cup opening upward will be transformed into the sound of trumpets. All growth will then resound with music. And as you learn to listen to nature even more deeply you will learn that the resonance of growth and development is an echo.

"The real music resounds in the cosmos. The sun and the stars resound; you hear the music of the planets and understand how they are calling the plants. Every opening blossom is a little sun; every plant twining its way upward a planetary revolution. Look at a tree: its whole being resounds. The sound of the tonic rumbles muffled in the solid trunk. The interval of the second resounds where the tree first divides, where it first branches out. And so it goes on. But most plants finish with the interval of the fifth. If you want to find a sixth or seventh you have to listen to the sounds which occur when the blossoms open delicately and the insects carry the pollen away to other plants. The new seed is the octave.

"The whole cosmos is music, and I listen to it year after year without ever tiring of it. Nothing in the cosmos which is repeated is ever quite the same. So every year, every century, has its own music."

"That is wonderful," said the youth. "Allow me to become your pupil and learn from you."

"I cannot teach you anything," the old man replied. "Your soul is much richer than mine. But I can teach you who your teachers are."

"And who are my teachers?" the youth asked in surprise.

"The cosmos itself," the old man told him. "The only reason you met me was to recognize the poverty of the people of my century. You will enrich them. But look, a bluebell. Observe it closely. Do you see its blue mantle? Protectively it is wrapped around a small yellow light within. This flower is an image of the soul. It, too, carries the light of the spirit within. It must never be extinguished. A blue mantle surrounds this light to prevent it from being extinguished. You also wore such a mantle before your mother conceived you. Keep it in your consciousness."

The old man also had a good relationship with animals. No animal was afraid of him. They trusted him and did not run away when he approached. And if they were ill or wounded they came to him to be healed. The old man knew which herbs healed which injuries and he also knew the proper time to pick the herbs. The healing properties of one might be brought about by the waxing moon when the sap rises like the tide; another would gain its strength through its fiery, aromatic properties with a waning moon when the sap was held back like the tide at ebb.

The young knight learned all this with the feeling that it was something that he had known before. On one occasion he dreamed about the old man; he, the youth, was old and the old man was young. He saw himself as the teacher and the old man as his pupil. The more the young knight experienced these things, the more of a riddle they became.

Here we have to pause. In profound words Walter Johannes Stein speaks here of the secret of the relation between teacher and pupil. During this conversation the young knight, Schionatulander, experiences a retrospect into a prior life, when the pupil had been the teacher of the old man! In the current life, the old Trevrezent leads the youth through the kingdoms of nature and awakens latent capacities in him. In this the old man takes on a serving role.

But in this learning process a new step is taken. The moment has come when the youth asks, out of his own inner knowing, what follows after "learning to read the book of nature." This leads teacher and pupil into the realm of the Seven Liberal Arts and, at the same time, it is a step in the unveiling of the mystery of the Grail.

One day he asked the old man, who seemed to be in a communicative mood: "Tell me, how do you know so much?"

"Nature has taught me," the old man said, "its great textbook is inexhaustible."

"No," cried the youth, "you are hiding something. You also know the subjects taught in our schools. You are more than a hermit, you have learnt more in the past."

The old man said: "Now I know that the hour of parting has come. I will tell you who your teachers are because they were mine as well. But once you have heard it you will leave. And rightly so. You only met me to go on and discover other things. So listen:

"Dialectic is taught in the schools. No one knows who taught this subject first. But I will tell you: it is none other than the Moon.* Observe it as it traverses the sky. It does not look at anything from one side only. It looks at everything from all sides. Do likewise. Do not think you know everything and can therefore rest. No, look alertly around you. Everything will look different tomorrow.

"Furthermore, learn from the Moon. Observe how it has reduced its fullness since yesterday. It consumes itself as it revolves. Learn that lesson and you will understand when I say that the Moon was my teacher. Happy the man who can subsume his own opinion in the art of dialectic and learn something better. Happy the man who makes his own light disappear, like the Moon, in order to receive and reflect illumination from the more exalted sun. Let the Moon teach you reflection. Then your knowledge will continue to wax after it has first waned. Are you not aware of the words of John, who baptized Jesus? He said: 'He must increase while I must decrease.' He was a master

---

*The Seven Liberal Arts are not listed here in their classical sequence. According to *De Nuptiis Philologiae et Mercurii* by Martianus Capella, a widely known textbook in the Middle Ages, the sequence was: grammar, dialectic, rhetoric, geometry, arithmetic, astronomy, *harmonia* (music). In the present case the sequence is determined by the planetary spheres which the soul traverses after death.

of dialectic, as you can see from his words. He also gained his wisdom from the Moon. The Moon is a good teacher. None but Gabriel, who endows the Moon with its soul, has ever taught dialectic."

The young knight sat in silence beside the old man. The Moon slowly made its way through the branches of the giant trees in the forest. Thereupon the youth said to the old man: "So dialectic is selflessness?"

"Yes," the old man said, "that is it."

Then the old man spoke about the souls of those who have died, how they become fully selfless in the sphere of the Moon and thus are an archetypal image of this art. Think of all the inspiration we can find in this picture as teacher and parent! Being a teacher indeed means changing one's approach and discovering new points of view time and time again. Subject teaching strongly stimulates this process. Being a teacher becomes a true art in which the pupil has an awakening effect on the teacher.

The old Trevrezent tells young Schionatulander about seven teachers. First the old man spoke of the Moon and of Gabriel as the great teacher of Dialectic, the art of never ceasing to learn by observing again and again from changing points of view. And it is so effective when one always seeks new points of view and entry points into a subject. In the Waldorf high school, however, the teacher asks the pupils themselves to practice the art of Dialectic.

But there are six more teachers the pupil needs to know about. The conversation between young Schionatulander and old Trevrezent, as described in the lecture by Walter Johannes Stein, continues as follows:

The youth then asked: "Now, old man, reveal your knowledge of the whole progression to me. What can be learnt from Mercury?"

"Mercury is the sphere," the old man said, "in which the soul discards pictorial vision, separating itself from ordinary images. The only thing it can take into that sphere is non-pictorial thinking. If you want to live in this sphere you can do so through numbers. If you say: one apple, one pear, the apple and the pear are images in your mind.

But if you say one, two, three, you inhabit a non-pictorial world. Mercury or Hermes has always been the teacher of arithmetic to all the peoples. The Greeks called him the god of merchants, because these have to deal with figures. We, however, call him Raphael, the angel of healing. The art of healing is a secret arithmetic. Physicians always deal with the number three. Know then, that every number has its secret:

> One is the first, undivided entity
> Two is the contrast of polarities
> Three is the harmony between the poles
> Four reveals what is hidden
> Five is the number of decision
> Six the number of love
> Seven determines the totality of time
> Eight is the number of justice
> Nine is the number of the divine order
> Ten is the number of the human being.

"The Saviour was the third between the two tempters. The one tempter always wants too much, the other too little. The golden mean lies between too much and too little. On the golden path, foolhardiness is too much, cowardice is too little, courage is the golden mean.

"There are four realms of nature: mineral, plant, animal and human. There are also four elements: fire, air, water and earth. The *Quinta Essentia* is hidden. It is the true nature of light. In the physical world you can only see illuminated matter. In thinking, light itself is revealed to you: enlightenment, the flash of inspiration. Five is the dividing line. I taught you that when we spoke about the plant. A tree propagates or not, if its seeds fall on stony ground. Events can go in either direction.

"The number six belongs to the bees. They use it to build their combs. Here love is impersonal, devoted completely to the service of the whole. Seven is seen in the rainbow, the week. Eight is twice four: Divine and earthly justice. Nine is the divine choirs and ten represents human beings, for they are the tenth hierarchy."

Old Trevrezent then spoke of the work of the physician, how he always works with the number three and how healing is hidden in three. And think how healing arithmetic is when we approach it out of movement. It has a healing effect on the often overly heavy or overly light constitution of the children's limbs. An arithmetic lesson brings health, movement and cheerful lightness into the class. A good teacher can be mercurial.

We continue when Schionatulander asked the old man about Venus:

"And what does Venus teach us?" the youth asked.

The old man became sad when the youth asked this and said: "Hardly anyone has any notion of Venus. Only people who purify their will, who no longer carry any desire into this sphere, have proper access to it. All selfish thirst for action has to be extinguished here. One who succeeds in that recognizes what real will is: music, nothing but music. The musical element is the essence of objectified will. That is why Eros must be left behind if one would see the lady Venus naked and experience the most beautiful music in existence. No one has ever learnt music except from Venus. She changes the voice of human beings as they mature on earth. Anyone whose song is noble and pure also has to be selfless and loyal. Treachery and betrayal do not go with the noble art of singing."

The youth resolved to become a noble minstrel. He would journey through the woods with his lute and make the people noble and good. And then, perhaps, at a castle he would find the woman destined for him. But he wanted only someone who loved the stars. That is how he would recognize her.

The old man said: "The sun shines on things visible while light itself remains behind the world of the senses. Michael, the sun prince, remains hidden behind physical phenomena, as does light, but without him world evolution would have no meaning. Understand the meaning which rests hidden behind what is as clear as the sun and you will have learnt the cosmic script of Michael, and will become a student in the art of grammar. First you must learn to discover the letters. Every butterfly wing, the wing of every tiny ladybird will show you the letters of the cosmic script. All the mysterious symbols which are engraved on crystals and stones are his script. There is no butterfly wing on which the stars have not recorded their script. For the stars inscribe the flow of time into the things of this world. And Michael, the sun prince, rules the progress of time."

When the youth heard this he felt the urge for action; he wanted to become the defender of justice. "Master, I want to become a grammarian," he declared, "I want to engrave a letter myself of the cosmic script with my life."

In these sentences, reported to us by Walter Johannes Stein, Grammatica becomes grand and broad. It was no accident that Rudolf Steiner indicated the importance of grammar in education. By discovering the laws of grammar, we discover the order that is hidden in the external phenomenon of language. It stimulates us to look for the activities that order the world of phenomena and, at the same time, when we practice this art it gives us confidence in the world of observation and perception, and thus encourages us to act. Think of the joy we feel when we find the structures that were hidden at first sight, but are yet present in every sentence. Love for the language, the world of the word, grows and builds an inner "skeleton" in the soul of the child. It carries and forms the budding world of experience. Grammatica is truly a sun art.

To the youth's enthusiasm to become a grammarian the old man now replied: "You will, because you are destined to do so and your ardor will enable you to fulfill your vocation. Know then, that the most wonderful character is the bodily form. You will learn to engrave the form of your future body when you pass after death through the region of the Sun to approach the sphere of Mars. Mars is filled with activity. In its sphere you learn to draw the lines for future development. It is the teacher of geometry, but the geometry it teaches is not tedious; the lines it draws have to be conquered. Great generals are geometricians in the heavenly realms before they descend to do their deeds on earth."

The old man became filled with enthusiasm. He seemed to know more about this region than about the others. But the youth had not heard everything. He sat there pensively and said: "Love is stronger than hate, isn't it?"

It is so indeed," the old man answered.

"What does the soul experience in sleep?" the youth asked. "What does it see when it carries the light of consciousness into the darkness?"

"It sees how the soul itself works to restore the body," the old man said.

"Is the soul then in heaven among the stars?" the youth asked.

"It is. It builds the body according to the archetypes in the stars. When your body lies asleep, the soul weaves golden threads from ganglion to ganglion. It draws triangles and all kinds of shapes from the star pattern."

"So that is geometry," said the youth, "and Mars is its teacher?"

"Of course," the old man replied. "You build in the blood according to the archetype of these patterns."

"God, then, is always engaged in geometry," the youth said.

Deep secrets were told here by Trevrezent to his pupil. As the pupil wakes up to his own powers, he will unceasingly pose deepening questions, thus making the art of geometry visible in all its aspects. This art is practiced from the first day in the first grade of a Waldorf school. Together with the children, with whom they will have an intense connection for many years, teachers draw the first geometrical forms, archetypal forms: straight and curved.

In drawing the first forms of letters the teacher, step by step, walks a path that through many years of form drawing leads to geometry. Every week again, the straight and the curved are conquered anew in form drawing, and starting in sixth grade this path of exercises and practice finds its continuation in geometry. But greatest is the world that hides behind this art. How instructive are the words of the old man!

The youth continued: "Now teach me the art of Jupiter. I have learnt to create forms that can serve living things. But where does life stream into these forms?"

"That happens in the realm of Jupiter," the old man said. "On earth you are only aware of life in the form of thinking.* Thinking, and thus life, have their home in the sphere of Jupiter. It is the origin of life."

"But which is the art?" the youth cried, "Teach me the *art* of Jupiter."

"That is the art of speech," the old man said, "for rhetoric is the art of infusing the forms of Samael with life through the power of Zachariel. Mars forms the word in the air, but Jupiter fills it with life. Zachariel, the spirit of Jupiter, teaches you to enliven your words so that joy and well-being stream from them."

The teacher uses this art continually with the children in the class. His words want to bestow joy and health on them. O, how difficult it is always to find this life bestowing force, day in and day out! But how effective it is when this power of the word lives in the classroom!

"Now there is only sphere left," the old man continued. "It is the farthest one, Saturn. It is Oriphiel who embraces everything and forms its boundary. This is the sphere where the soul turns round after death. In the region of Mars the soul has refashioned the body to the form it should take in the next life. In the region of Jupiter it has prepared the new life which vitalizes the created form. Now, in the sphere of Saturn, it ensouls its creation. In its descent to earth, the soul will become filled with spirit and form a new ego-consciousness. Then it chooses the time and place of its birth in anticipation of its descent. At that point the soul learns the art of astronomy."

---

*The reference is to abstract, dead thinking tied to the brain, and to living, supersensible thinking, respectively.

Thus the youth also learned about the last of the Seven Liberal Arts. What gifts does this art have for us as parent or teacher? Astronomy, the knowledge of the stars, is one of the subjects taught in the Waldorf school. It explores the externally visible world of stars. But the Grail story acquaints us with a different way to approach the stars. This way is called the reading of the stellar script. What is one to read in the stellar script? It is a search for those people who will one day serve the Grail. In the stellar script the innate, completely individual impulse with which every human child is born, becomes visible. Just this is the riddle we face as parent and teacher. And in our task we search for the solution. Here we work out of the stellar script with the true astronomy so that it becomes the art of education and upbringing. The youth thanked the old man with the following words, with which I will conclude these quotations:

> "I thank you. You have taught me much because you have brought me true tidings of the seven arts that liberate the soul and the spirit from the body, which otherwise happens only in death. In life I learn to die and in death to live. The Seven Liberal Arts are one path."

I hope that this conversation between the old hermit Trevrezent and the young Schionatulander may contribute to a further search for, and working with, the Seven Liberal Arts in and around our Waldorf schools.

PART 2
THE VIRGINS OF THE GRAIL

The Virgins appear in a dream to the Three Kings as the seven-pointed star
that announces the birth of the "new human being."

3 Alanus ab Insulis and the Grail

Alanus ab Insulis, the famous teacher of the School of Chartres, wrote about the Seven Liberal Arts in his book *Anticlaudianus*. This book had the subtitle *On the Heavenly Creation of the New Human Being*.

Alanus is an enigmatic personality. During his life he received the honorary title of *Doctor Universalis*, but very little is known about his biography. For instance, it has always remained unknown whether he was ever ordained as a priest. He did live for a long time in the Cistercian monastery in Citeaux (France). When he died there in 1203, the following epitaph was written on his gravestone: "Little is the grave and brief is the time that Alanus sojourns here, he who knows of the numbers 2 and 7, and possesses all wisdom."

There are several pictures of Alanus. In one of them he looks more like a troubadour and knight than a scholarly monk. When he was young he suffered a sunstroke and had a remarkable experience; it was as if he saw himself in a form he did not have in his life at that time. He related the following about this:

> From the sign of the bull the star of Apollo, the sun, was burning.
> It shot its red-hot arrows at my head and brain.
> I sought shelter in the shade between trees and bushes.
> Zephyr, the cooling west wind, had mercy on me.
> The afternoon was soon blazing as in summer,
> But in the leafy tent I lay well protected.
>
> All at once Pythagoras appeared and approached me closely.
> Whether he was in the body, I don't know.
> And while I beheld this image of the initiate,
> I saw it filled with wondrous signs.
> Whether I beheld this image free of the body,
> Whether I was in a body-free state—God knows it, I knew it not.

From his forehead shines the art of Astronomy,
Grammatica orders his teeth in harmony,
Rhetorica bestows on his tongue the fair, flowering word,
While Dialectica glows on his lips as logic.

His mobile fingers show Arithmetica,
And sounds flow from his throat as Musica,
Geometria shines cautiously from his eyes.
I saw how his body concealed the seven arts.

In this spiritual experience Alanus' higher being is awakened, and he finds
new inner guidance. Pythagoras continues:

Pythagoras showed me his right hand,
In occult signs I read the script to the edge,
I watched and read what was written:
"I shall be your guide, follow me now!"

In this vision Alanus follows Pythagoras. In ancient Greece, Pythagoras
was viewed as one of the great initiates. He dwelled in Egypt for a long
time and in a war of conquest he was brought to Babylon where he
met Zoroaster, counselor to King Cyrus the Great. He became one of
Zoroaster's faithful pupils.

Zoroaster renewed the teaching of Zarathustra, the great founder
of the first Persian culture who, according to Plato, lived in the sixth
millennium BCE. The Zend Avesta contains a prophecy in which Zoroaster
announces that he will be born again and that his faithful pupils will be
able to find him again if they follow his golden star. The name Zoroaster
means "Golden Star." Rudolf Steiner, in his spiritual-scientific research,
found that Pythagoras re-appeared as one of the three wise men who
visited and adored the newly born Jesus child in Bethlehem after they had
followed the "Golden Star."

Alanus was very familiar with the image of the Golden Star. In the
Cathedral in Chartres, the Golden Star appears in a special way. In the left
arch of the North Portal, the three wise men are shown sleeping together

under a blanket, and above them shines a seven-pointed golden star surrounded by a powerful wave-like movement. This seven-pointed golden star is a direct representation of the Seven Liberal Arts which Alanus had seen in his vision of Pythagoras.

Immediately before he was reborn, the being of Zoroaster showed itself as a star, but also as a kind of flower of great vitality. In the Jesus child described by St. Matthew, Zoroaster appeared anew in order to prepare the incarnation of Christ at the baptism in the Jordan.

Zoroaster taught the insight of the great Sun Spirit as the mighty aura of the sun: Ahura Mazdao. He described seven Amshaspands who serve the great Sun Spirit and enable the sun powers to work on the earth. They are connected with Sun, Moon, Mercury, Venus, Mars, Jupiter and Saturn. The Seven Liberal Arts have the same connections with the moving heavenly bodies that can be seen with the naked eye.

In later times, Titurel built the Grail Castle so as to give the Grail mysteries a place on earth. Titurel, a legendary figure, was born in the north of Spain. The Grail was kept protected in the castle that he built there, far removed from the inhabited world. Parzival, the Grail seeker, finally found it after long trials and wanderings. When he was called to the Grail, he was accompanied by the spiritual forces of the seven planets that are seen with the inner eye as the seven virgins of the liberal arts. They are the same as the Grail virgins who, together with others, make initiation in the mystery of the Grail possible.

Alanus ab Insulis knew this path. And the fact that in his epitaph it says that he knew the secrets of the two and the seven means that he was initiated in the mystery of the Grail. The secret of the seven he knew like no other in the path through the Seven Liberal Arts. The secret of the two is the secret of good and evil as it is told in the Grail legend as the struggle between Klingsor and the guardians of the moral power of the Grail.

An initiate in the Grail was called a Parzival. In this sense, Alanus was a Parzival.[14]

When we summarize all of this we see that Alanus met Pythagoras during a spiritual experience, and that he saw on his body the qualities of the

Seven Liberal Arts. Pythagoras was a pupil of Zoroaster who taught the secret of seven as Ahura Mazdao and the seven serving Amshaspands. Pythagoras was reborn as one of the three wise men who followed the seven-pointed Golden Star and found their reborn teacher Zoroaster in Bethlehem.

And then, again according to Rudolf Steiner, Zoroaster reappeared as Titurel, the builder of the Grail Castle.[15] He is the great leader of the initiation in the Grail mystery. His pupils have the name Parzival. Alanus has a deep connection with this path through the Grail mysteries. It is entirely possible that in Pythagoras, Alanus was experiencing his own being in the time of Zoroaster.

But the vision of Alanus is not yet finished:

> Pythagoras glided before me so that I could hardly follow him
> And quicker than my speech was our flight
> Away to another land;
> It showed me many wonders and people in innumerable masses.
> Here is Pricianus who (as grammarian) may use the cane with strictness,
> And Aristotle (the dialectician) who drives the demons away with blows,
> While Cicero (the rhetorician) selects the prettiest words.
> Ptolemy directs himself to the starry world,
> Boëthius on all that can be counted.
> Euclid is also here; he measures the space (as a geometrical artist).
> Pythagoras is here and goes in and out like a smith,
> Until in his hammering he sounds tones in music.*

---

*Pricianus (ca. 500 CE), Latin grammarian
Aristotle (384–322 BCE), Greek philosopher
Marcus Tullius Cicero (106–43 BCE), Roman philosopher, statesman, lawyer, orator
Claudius Ptolemaeus (90–168 CE), Greco-Roman mathematician, astronomer/astrologer, geographer
Anicius Manlius Severinus Boëthius (480–525 CE), Roman philosopher
Euclid (ca 300 BCE), Greek mathematician, the "father of geometry"
Pythagoras (570–495 BCE), Greek philosopher, mathematician, musician

In this spirit land Alanus met historical personalities as representatives and practitioners of the Seven Liberal Arts. They accompanied him on a spiritual path that ultimately led to the gates of heaven. During his initiation in the Grail mystery, Parzival had experienced these gates when he entered the Grail Castle.

> Suddenly, when I left the crowd in admiration,
> An angel approached me in speedy flight
> And spoke to me: "Open your eyes and look up,
> And see what moves in its speedy course.
> And while in fright I looked up to heaven
> I was suddenly taken into the spiritual world
> And I found myself standing before the heavenly gates.[16]

4 The Grail Castle and the Seven Liberal Arts

When Alanus had his spiritual experience he was transported to a world which he described extensively in his *Anticlaudianus*. Let us follow him again on his spiritual path. We will discover that his path corresponds in many respects with that of Parzival on his search for the Grail. Alanus' story is as follows:*

The realm of Natura.
The artist and goddess Natura has enriched many with her gifts, but now she wishes to achieve in one work a union of all that she had shared. It is to be the crown on her work and will overcome all one-sidedness. The anvil is insufficient for this work and Natura cannot even complete it by herself. She does not lose herself in laborious work but uses her intelligence to consider the individual challenges of the work.

Then she quickly calls her companions together for joint deliberation. Out of this joint deliberation insight will have to be born. A heavenly council is convened and the best entities from the heavenly spheres descend and illuminate the entire sphere of earth with their presence. The earth rejoices and the honor thus bestowed makes this burden light.

Natura dwells in a realm where the arts and virtues of the human being originate. She is surrounded by many virgins who each represent a particular virtue.

The heavenly council.
All have now come together in this council. Concord, the foster child of Peace, is first to get under way. Then comes Plenty pouring all

---

*From: Alanus ab Insulis, *Anticlaudianus*. In this chapter, Alanus' extensive, poetic original text has been condensed by F.L. into abbreviated descriptions, tr. by P.M. The complete book is available in English translation: Alan of Lille, *Anticlaudianus*, tr. James J. Sheridan, Toronto 1973.

sorts of things from a full horn. Favor, Youth bedecked with many a grace; Laughter that banishes the gloomy clouds from our minds; Temperance, Moderation, content within set limits; Reason, the measure of good, to her Honesty ever clings and accompanies her with joyous tread. Decorum; Prudence weighing all things in her scales. Discernment, Compassion and Truth know true Love and are able to distinguish her from deceit. The last companion is Nobility, of beautiful stature, who justly carries her fame. All of this heavenly youth hastens to the castle of Natura. The house is illumined by their radiance.

Around the year 1200 when Alanus wrote the account of his spiritual experience, the troubadours Chretien de Troyes and Wolfram von Eschenbach[17] were writing their stories of Parzival's search for the Holy Grail. In these stories about the knight Parzival, the virtues play an important role. The young Parzival wants to become a knight. One day, when he is hunting in a forest, he runs into some knights:

The lad asked: "You speak of knights. What is that? If you do not have God's kind of power, then tell me: who bestows knighthood?" "That King Arthur does. Young Sir, if you come to his house, he will give you the name of knight so that you will never need to be ashamed of it. You may well be of knightly race." And by the warriors he was scrutinized, and God's handiwork was manifest in him.—I have this from the adventure, with which truth was told me so. Never had a man's beauty been more nobly realized since Adam's time, and hence his praise was wide among women.[18]

Parzival is described here as a human being who is related to Adam. The knights from King Arthur see in Parzival something of the paradisal state of the human being.

But Parzival wants to move on; he wants to acquire knightly virtues. He goes on his way and, to become a knight of King Arthur, he has to develop the virtues of knighthood. Gurnemanz becomes his first teacher.

In the story of Alanus, the virgins in the realm of Natura are the ones who bring the virtues to the knights. The virgins of the virtues bestow joy on the soul and goodness and health on the life body. They are the givers of the life force. But they are also the Grail virgins who guard and carry the Grail in the Grail Castle. Natura herself is like Repanse de Schoye, the virgin who carries the Grail itself on an emerald green cloth.

The castle.
Natura's residence is magnificent. Nature here is eternally young. The roses bloom all year long, birds sing like heavenly sirens, and in the center a spring bubbles up from the ground. This spring is the beginning of a silvery stream that bestows the strength on the trees to grow the most delicious fruits.

The house of Natura is situated in a high place, above the wild tempests of the earth. Into the realm of air it is carried by pillars; from far away one can see sparkling precious stones and glistening silver and gold.

Imaginations are real.
Imagination, picture consciousness, provides proof, while logic must fight and defend. In this realm Aristotle defends and Plato proves. Here the power of imagination and the intellect are in balance.

Everything that receives but a part of the gifts of Natura, and also everything that withdraws from her art, is shown here in fables and images.

Here Natura reigns. Here she creates forms out of the past and has prophetic visions of the future. Here she connects with knots and numbers the elements of the earth, oceans, winds, earthquakes, the seasons and the fall of the snow. She harmoniously brings together fire, earth, air and water.

The castle of Natura was situated in the realm of the creative life forces. In the story of Parzival we also see that the Grail Castle stood on a high place on the boundary of heaven and earth. "Thus he rode up the mountain until he came to the top. When he arrived there he could look far in all directions and saw in front of him nothing but earth and heaven."[19]

Grail Castle (scenery used in the first performance of Richard Wagner's opera *Parsifal*)

Natura's cry of distress.

Natura takes the floor when the heavenly choir has filled the hall. Thoughtfully she inclines her head to the earth. "A work we must accomplish: the divine human being as the remedy for the many faults that have arisen from human one-sidedness. With his spirit the human being inhabits heaven, with his body the earth. He can only tread the middle way in virtue and in balance between the extremes." Natura lives in the sphere of earth. She creates and weaves and bestows natural forces onto everything. But spiritual power must descend to earth for the work to have a future—it appears in the human being as the Christ.

The distress of Natura is like that of the Grail virgin Repanse de Schoye who carries the Grail into the great hall, bringing its content as the remedy for the wounded Grail King Amfortas. Amfortas suffers from a wound he received through his own faults. Repanse de Schoye does not appear alone, but enters the hall accompanied by six other virgins:

> *Ah vois!* Six more are now seen coming arrayed in costly garb, one-half with a silk that was interwoven with gold, the rest of pfellel-silk from Nineveh. ... After them came the queen. So radiant was her countenance that everyone thought the dawn was breaking. She was clothed in a dress of Arabian silk. Upon a deep green achmardi she bore the perfection of Paradise, both root and branch. That was a thing called the Grail, which surpasses all earthly perfection. Repanse de Schoye was the name of her whom the Grail permitted to be its bearer. Such was the nature of the Grail that she who watched over it had to preserve her purity and renounce all falsity. Before the Grail came lights of no small worth, six vessels of clear glass, tall and beautifully formed, in which balsam was burning sweetly.[20]

In Alanus' description, the virgins of the Seven Liberal Arts have the task of connecting the human being with the earth in the right way. They are like Repanse de Schoye with the six virgins who bring in the Grail to bestow new life forces on the wounded King Amfortas. With the power of the Grail they also preserve the life of the old master builder of the Grail Castle, Titurel.

But let us now continue the story of Alanus and hear how the virgins of the Seven Liberal Arts build a chariot in order to travel to higher spiritual realms so that a new human being, akin to Adam, may be conducted to the earth as the most virtuous knight.

The helping Seven Liberal Arts.
If the human being is to correctly connect himself with the earth, he has to be carried from the heavenly realms of the Divine Trinity to the earth in the chariot that was built by the Seven Liberal Arts.

Grammatica fashions the pole of the chariot. Dialectic makes the axle, and Rhetorica decorates the pole with precious stones and silver, and chisels flowers into the axle. Arithmetica builds the first wheel from marble, Musica forges the second wheel from bronze, Geometria makes the third wheel from lead and Astronomia forges the fourth wheel from gold. The intellect puts five horses to the chariot with which Prudentia (wisdom) will go and fetch the spirit for the new human being from God. The horses are the senses: sight, hearing, smell, taste and touch.

In the *Anticlaudianus*, virtues are bestowed upon the heavenly human being when he descends to the earth in the chariot of the soul, built by the Seven Liberal Arts.

When Prudentia reaches the world of the nine hierarchies she is transformed into Phronesis—the one who has achieved inspired knowledge through the power of her heart, the sober one. When she is able to appear before God she becomes Sophia, the wise one. Then she brings the spirit for the new human being back to the earth.

Alanus knows this new human being, who is the same as the one who in the epic of his contemporary, Wolfram von Eschenbach, becomes known to all as Parzival.

5 Grammatica: The Art of the Creative Word[21]

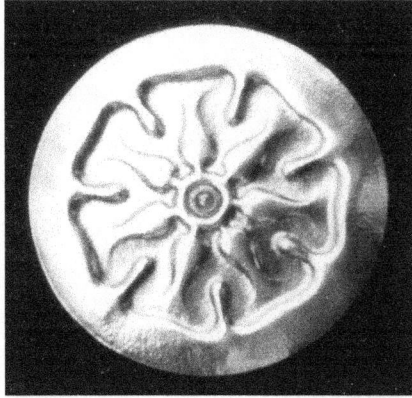

The Virgin

The first one among the liberal arts is the Virgin Grammatica. Martianus Capella described her as the inspiring power behind the practice of grammar.

In the famous school of Chartres, the process of learning was experienced as an encounter with this inspiring soul force. In each of the seven subjects of learning a spiritual being is present; she is invisible but can be experienced. This is how Martianus Capella described the Virgin Grammatica:

> Grammatica is the eldest of the seven sisters which Apollo gives
> as wedding presents to Philologia, the earthly bride of his brother
> Mercury.
>
> So Latona's son [Apollo] moved forward from her former place
> as one of the servants of Mercury, an old woman indeed but of great
> charm, who said that she had been born in Memphis [Egypt] when
> Osiris was still king. When she had been a long time in hiding, she
> was found and brought up by the Cyllenian [Mercury] himself. This
> woman claimed that in Attica [Greece], where she had lived for the

greater part of her life, she moved about in Greek dress. But because of the Latin gods and the Capitol and the race of Mars and descendants of Venus, according to Roman custom, she entered the senate of the gods dressed in a Roman cloak. She carried in her hands a polished box, a fine piece of cabinetmaking, which shone on the outside with light ivory, from which, like a skilled physician, the woman took out the emblems of wounds that need to be healed. Out of this box she took first a pruning knife with a shining point, with which she said she could prune the faults of pronunciation in children; then they could be restored to health with a certain black powder carried through reeds, a powder which was thought to be made of ash or the ink of cuttlefish. Then she took out a very sharp medicine which she had made of fennel flower and the clippings from a goat's back, a medicine of purest red color.

How may we understand the being of this virgin, the first one of the liberal arts?

Daughter of Osiris

The reference by this virgin to the time when Osiris was still king takes us back to mythological times. In primeval civilizations, which Egyptian priests placed in the age of Atlantis, the being of Osiris was in all concrete reality working on earth.[22] It is an early period in human development, the time when the capacity of speech and the use of language were acquired by the human being.

Seven centuries after Martianus Capella, Alanus ab Insulis also wrote that the Virgin Grammatica came from Egypt. He described her as dressed in a garment made of Egyptian papyrus.[23] She came into the world in Memphis during the reign of Osiris, and was found and raised by Hermes Trismegistus who was called Mercury by the Romans. Her garment is covered with an indelible script for she is connected with the capacity of writing and thus with the destiny of Osiris. Osiris represents the pure sun force which lives in the human being as the power of imagination.

When Osiris withdrew, Hermes protected this power and during the time of the Egyptian cultural epoch he developed it further as the art

The Virgin Grammatica with Donatus

of Grammatica. He spread the story of Osiris who was lured and locked into a lead sarcophagus by Typhon. The legend describes here how the imaginative power of the word dies in hieroglyphics, in ever more abstract characters, in lead. This death process of Osiris found its ultimate end in the art of printing which works with lead letters.

The Virgin Grammatica still preserves some of the protective, creative power of language which once lived in Osiris.

Gift from Odin

In the northern parts of Europe a different divinity was connected with language. It is Odin, also called Wotan, the All-Father. He was the first to bestow on humanity the magically working power of the word, and later the script in the form of the runes.

Just as in the story of Osiris the divine word is rigidified in a lead sarcophagus, here we also find a description of the process of the transformation of sound into letter. Grammatica points to this process, in which sounds are changed into written signs that can be read.

The formative power of the word

In the description by Alanus, the Virgin Grammatica bestows milk on her pupils as a nourishing life force. But at the same time, she carries in her hand a cane. She is strict and permits no disorder but, on the other hand, she freely gives this vivifying milk. In the small child this milk engenders activity. At the time of the change of teeth the formative life forces are freed as the power which makes it possible for the child to learn in its own way.

The Virgin Grammatica has bright white teeth; she removes all tartar and caries from her teeth with a scraper.

Teeth and grammar

The human being observes with the senses and articulates with the use of the incisors. In their function they are related to the nouns in the language. The molars are invisible to the eye but they work with great force. They fully transform the food we take in. They are the workers, like the verbs in the language. The eyeteeth form the harmonious transition between incisors and molars. They are not in the forefront, and they have a quality that corresponds with that of an adjective or an adverb.

The Virgin Grammatica speaks clearly and beautifully with her ivory-white teeth. The power of the word is freed when in the child the teeth have been formed. The child then speaks without lisping and with clear articulation.

Three types of words

Nouns – In the practice of grammar we discover by means of the nouns the multiplicity of forms, not only in the language but in the world. We name things: rose, horse, sun, home; but also properties of the soul such as love, friendship, hate. We acknowledge the world in its many forms. The word *substantivum*, Latin for *noun*, indicates the property of substance.

Adjectives – In the adjectives we express the quality of the things, events and experiences we name as nouns.

Verbs – In the verb we experience the principle of working, of activity in the world. It is expressed in the first sentence of the Gospel of St. John: "In the beginning was the [creative] Word."

Grammatica and the virtue of justice

The old alchemist, Basil Valentine, places the practice of this art in relation to the virtue of justice, who is often depicted as *Justitia* carrying a pair of scales. She represents the condition of equilibrium between anarchy and dictatorship. She protects society from arbitrariness or tyranny through her awareness of right. It is also a virtue that the practitioner of Grammatica acquires as a life habit.

Moreover, the virtue of justice is dependent on exact observation connected with clear and orderly thinking. Notably it is exact observation that is the result of Grammatica. For this reason, Alanus concludes his description of the Virgin Grammatica with the following words: "Thus she preserves the sequence of images in the art, and she is for our eyes like a refreshing drink, as a greeting with which she attends to the needs of the table of our spirit."

Grail secret

Here the Grail secret is expressed. The purest sense impressions are connected with clear thinking in the head, which is receptive and pure like the Grail vessel: "For an important painter has designed the images; and yet the clear sense impressions are praised more in him than the painter expected."

The revelation of the threefold sun

Grammatica is the first art that is practiced in the framework of the Seven Liberal Arts. In grammar we have a direct encounter with the formative forces of the sun as these come to expression in the language. We name the creative force of life, and thus of the sun, which works directly into matter as the formative principle. It is this formative power that is described at the beginning of the Gospel of St. John as the Logos, the World Word.

How can we gain access to this creative process? When we listen to language we experience in its sounds, words and sentences a grandiose dimension which works in conversation, in dialogue. It is no accident that Plato wrote his philosophical insights in the form of dialogues. In dialogue, the creative process of language can be experienced directly. A similar process takes place in a poet who uses the language to create words that are alive.

The poet is bound by the constitution of the language being within which he works. This constitution consists of the sentences, and their construction and relationships. Related sentences form paragraphs. Sentences can be indicative, questioning, imperative or descriptive; they may have an active, creative or a more receptive or passive nature. As word-creators in dialogue we enter the realm of the being of the language, and we have to learn how to handle it. This is also true for the relationships of the words and clauses in the sentence. Every part of the sentence and every word has its own particular character.

In the words, the creative process of the language ends. It is as if the formative power of the language is crystallized into the words. In this way, the words are like the condensed and crystallized minerals of the earth.

What kinds of words are there? Words that name something; they separate things into individual items: birch, sun, light. There are also words that indicate activity, such as to think, to feel, to will, to hear and to become. They have a quality of transformation.

Then there are words that express the quality of things. They often occur in relation to things that can be named, such as: a clear crystal, a six-pointed star, the young child. These words are not just additive; rather they enable us to experience quality. Words can also indicate the quality of an activity: he speaks well, she paints beautifully.

Thus we see that words that name things have a static, recognizable character. In the human being this naming takes place with the help of thinking, which has its seat in the head. By contrast, activity is stimulated primarily from the human limbs; it is indicated by the verbs. In between we see the adjectives; they add quality to the objects recognized and named through thinking and to the deeds formed by the will. The adjectives are related to feeling (the heart). This is shown in the drawing below.

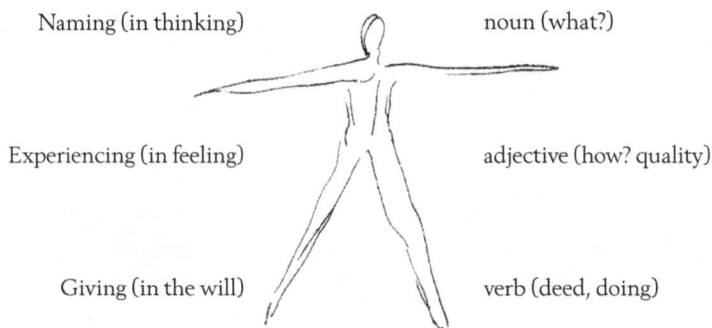

Naming (in thinking) — noun (what?)

Experiencing (in feeling) — adjective (how? quality)

Giving (in the will) — verb (deed, doing)

More than anything else, grammar has to do with the mutual relationships of words and clauses within the sentence. Is there a just relationship between the realms of will, feeling and thinking in the sentence?

Beyond the different types of words we have to deal with sentence construction. How do the subject and the verb relate? Is it a just relationship? Is it asking for an object or indirect object?

Language analysis

In language there is a hidden structure that the modern science of grammar attempts to recognize. The sources of language forming forces are investigated in the modern philosophy of language, often with the help of Anglo-Saxon ways of language analysis. Ludwig Wittgenstein, a contemporary of Rudolf Steiner, is recognized as one of the pioneers in this field.

The modern approach of language scientists is based on observation and analysis. In scientific practice in the Middle Ages, language was still viewed as an artistic process, and therefore a process of creation.

Virtue

The Liberal Art of Grammatica is a path of exercise and practice toward justice (Justitia). Grammar is about giving words and clauses their proper places in the sentence. Transgressions can be committed here. Therefore the question of justice is an appropriate one, and strictness is necessary.

Donatus as teacher *

In the sculptures of the Cathedral in Chartres, Grammatica is accompanied by Donatus, who wrote the *Ars Grammatica* in Rome about 400 CE. By the way, all sculptured virgins on the Cathedral of Chartres are accompanied by masculine teachers at their feet.

Exercise
The practice of grammar can become surprisingly fascinating when we are able to raise this sometimes dry and analytical subject to the level of art, in

---

*Aelius Donatus (fourth century CE) was a Roman grammarian. The only fact known regarding his life is that he was the tutor of St. Jerome.

a creative process. The following exercise can help with this. The exercise may be performed either alone or in a group.

Draw a triangle on a sheet of paper.
- Write a verb above the top of the triangle, either an infinitive or conjugation, e.g., *sparkle.*
- By the right hand angle write a noun that goes with the verb, such as *stars.*
- By the left hand angle write an adjective, e.g., *clear.*

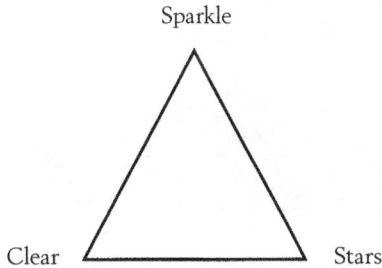

The next step consists in making a sentence that we write around the triangle. Use the words that are already there and add other words in between. Indicate with a capital where the sentence begins and by a dot, exclamation point or question mark where it ends.

    Example: The clear stars sparkle in radiant beauty.
    Or: Clear crystals sparkle like stars.
    Or: Stars sparkle in the clear sky.

When we do this exercise in a group, and the verb, noun and adjective have been written down, we hand the paper on to the next person after the addition of every new word.

The last person, who writes down the entire sentence, then hands the paper back to the first person who had drawn the triangle and written down the verb. It is the verb that has called forth the creative activity, and now the creator receives the sentence back as a gift.

It can be great fun to do this exercise together with others because of the surprising talents that often come to light.

6 Rhetorica: The Art of the Spoken Word

The Virgin

Rhetorica appears as a virgin of tall stature, full of self-confidence and of an extraordinary beauty with rosy cheeks. She wears a helmet wreathed in royal symbols. In her hands she has weapons with which she can defend herself, but also wound her enemies. She radiates with the power of lightning. The garments she wears under her armor are covered with a cloak wrapped around her shoulders after the Roman custom. The cloak shines with the light of many images of plans and inventions. On her breast she wears an ornament that sparkles with jewels of the most exquisite colors.

When she beats her armor with her weapons, thunderclaps roll through the space, accompanied by lightning bolts. Indeed, she resembles Jupiter in the way she throws lightning and thunder through space. But what calm and self-control she exudes, and how perfect is the lofty power of the words she uses! (After Martianus Capella)

Eloquence

Rhetorica shows her eloquence, an art she has mastered like no one else. She laughs more than anyone. But tears may also moisten her cheeks, yet on the rosy red of her colorful face they quickly dry up into a smile. The heights and depths of her soul are shown in her eyes. Alanus says that she is stately, has rosy cheeks and a noble, self-assured nature. Like Martianus Capella and Alanus ab Insulis, Adelard of Bath also describes Rhetorica as a fair maiden. In the sequence in which I present the Trivium, I follow that of Adelard of Bath in his treatise *De Eodem et Diverso* (*Of Similarities and Differences*).

Rhetorica's robe is multi-colored and full of the most magnificent images. Alanus says that she is a master in the art of painting. She paints with words, and just like her robe she herself is full of images.

Fighting spirit

In Alanus' work Rhetorica is described as carrying two instruments: on her right a tuba and on her left a horn. They resound when Rhetorica stands before the throne of Zeus, says Martianus Capella. It is as if she uses them to announce a battle.

She can throw words like lightning and thundering threats, but can also besiege you with entreaties or bless you with praise. She uses questions to light upon the right arguments so she can form the judgment with which she will build the content that enables her to reach her goal. She orders the arguments into a composition and with her good memory does not forget what is important. She speaks in a well-formed way with the right intonation and sound in order to move the souls of those who listen and must come to a judgment, and to carry them along with her artful arguments. Her gestures also greatly assist her.

Organization

She knows how to arrange the organization of the discourse to serve its goal and content. The beginning, the prologue, has to prick the listeners' ears. A story has to engender an experience of what is true, and must

The Virgin Rhetorica
with Cicero

hide potential errors: healing by the image of truth. The synopsis that follows unifies the parts. (Today the synopsis often precedes the body of the discourse.) In an oration, what is expounded is united in one great movement to result in a pronouncement substantiated by arguments. In conclusion, the Virgin Rhetorica will recapitulate her reasoning and arguments.

In the court of law

Thus she keeps a tight rein on herself to achieve her purpose during the oration. In the court of law the judges seek the right judgment. In contrast with old Germanic law, Roman law is written down in codes of law. In Germanic law, dialogue and discussion on the *Thingplatz* (the assembly and court of law) were the basis on which a sound judgment was reached. Even the Christian priests spoke to the people in Germanic countries on the *Thingplatz.* That meant that their oratorical skills were of great importance.

Rhetorica and the feeling life

In rhetoric, the listeners are awakened from the middle realm, the feeling and experiencing part of the human being, so as to follow the speaker through thinking and to support the judgment through the will. The human middle, the human feeling, forms the entry point for Rhetorica, and from there she moves between thinking and the will. She stands and works in the horizontal plane, just as Grammatica works in the vertical. In doing so, Rhetorica raises great inner movements of joy and sorrow, struggle and rest.

People and nations

Who are the ones fighting each other when peoples do not understand each other? Battles between peoples may be expressions of a mutual lack of understanding of the folk signature and thus of the identity, as this is carried by folk spirits from the ranks of the archangels.

Rhetorica brings its practitioners within the reach of their folk spirits through the language. A folk spirit belongs to the rank of the archangels. Good speaking creates during sleep a good connection with the archangels. Speaking materialistically hinders, while speaking spiritually engenders a connection with the folk and language spirit. In the night inspiration is born. When we consciously handle language and poetic inspiration received during the night, we create a favorable condition for a conscious collaboration with the archangel through the consciousness of inspiration.

Development of language in children

Just like Grammatica, Rhetorica has a direct connection with the first speech of a child. In Adelard of Bath's work, the arts of Grammatica and Rhetorica follow each other. There is a correspondence here with the sequence of development in the child, which leads from walking to speaking. At a later age, the Virgins Rhetorica and Grammatica lead us to rediscover the initial achievements of the child and become active in their metamorphosis.

Rhetorica and the virtues of courage and hope

Rhetorica also brings a virtue into being in the soul life of the human being. It is the future-oriented power of courage (*fortitudo*) which Rhetorica awakens in human soul life through her effective orations.

Courage is a quality that is called upon in battle. It often determines the outcome of the battle. The force of weapons can be curbed by courageous words. A courageous deed can save lives. The battle is always creatively engaged when the virtue of courage is present.

It always makes us feel good when someone speaks an encouraging word to us in a difficult life situation. Sometimes we need courage to speak out, and it requires courage to give a lecture to an audience.

Cicero as teacher

In connection with Rhetorica, both Alanus ab Insulis and Martianus Capella wrote about Roman law and based themselves especially on

Cicero's *Inventiones*.* On the West Portal of Chartres Cathedral, Cicero appears right beside Rhetorica.

Exercise 1
- Form a circle.
- A person who is willing and can muster the courage begins with telling a story.
- When this person stops, the next person has the floor.
- The new speaker tries to continue the story but is also free to give it a new turn.
- When everyone has had a turn, the person who started the story tries to give a strong ending.
- After the story is finished, it is reviewed by the group. Try to form an overview of its development and to arrive at an insight into the composition and content. This can be done very well in the form of a listening conversation in which every contribution should be respected.

This exercise produces amazing results and is wonderful to do. In the process, everyone develops the courage to tell something. The threshold is low because a contribution may consist of just a couple of sentences or may also be much longer.

Exercise 2
In the Middle Ages the art of discourse was often practiced in rhetoric. Alanus ab Insulis was clear and concise when he described the construction of a good discourse:

> *How to give form to a discourse*
> The beginning, the **prologue**, brings the spirit into movement so that the ears are pricked and hearing is sharpened. This wins the hearts of critical spirits so that the listener becomes more attentive and positive, and begins to show a willingness to learn.

---

*Marcus Tullius Cicero (106–43 BCE) was a Roman philosopher, statesman, lawyer, orator, political theorist, consul and constitutionalist.

65

Then the actual **discourse** sketches the truth in brief characteristics. The untrue is, in this phase, hidden under the image of the true.

The **synopsis** then connects the parts. Everything that was described in the discourse as separate points of view is brought together again.

The phase of the **conclusion**, which includes a judgment, also contains a terse review of the arguments of the synopsis.

At the **close**, the goal of the discourse is once again clearly formulated. The speaker is like a horseman who pulls the reins of his horse so as to reach his goal.[24]

Alanus thus distinguishes five elements in the construction of a speech. Prologue – discourse – synopsis – conclusion and close– closely follow each other in sequence. When we take a closer look at this construction, we will discover that Alanus created an organic whole. In order to stand firmly in life, the following five capacities play a basic role:

> Steadfastness
> Security
> Love
> Hope
> Trust

In the first part of the discourse, the *prologue*, and also in the *synopsis*, steadfastness and an inner sense of security can, as virtues of the speaker, awaken in the listener the willingness to follow him in his thoughts. Love is the virtue the speaker has to develop in himself for the subject he presents in the body of his *discourse*. Hope and trust impart the necessary power of conviction to the *conclusion* and the *close*.

Exercise 3
Rudolf Steiner presented an exercise for spiritually striving people to develop and strengthen these five basic capacities. It is best to do this exercise in the morning (and also preceding a lecture or public speech).

Steadfastly I stand upon the earth   (concentrate on left leg)
With certainty I walk the road of life   (concentrate on right leg)
Love I carry in the core of my being   (concentrate on left arm)
Hope flows into all my deeds   (concentrate on right arm)
Trust guides my thinking   (concentrate on head)

One concludes the exercise with the following two lines:

These five take me to my goal
These five give me life on earth.[25]

This exercise has an inner relationship with the five elements Alanus described for the construction of a virtuous address. The being of the Virgin Rhetorica is strengthened by this exercise in her own art of speech.

In a diagram it might look as shown below:

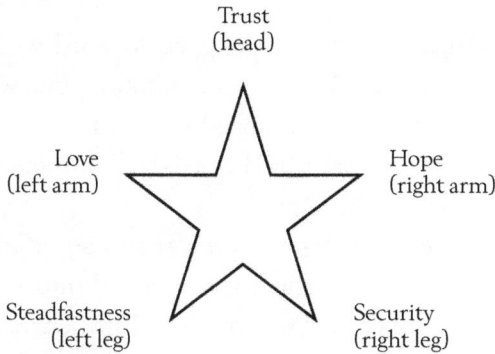

Trust
(head)

Love
(left arm)

Hope
(right arm)

Steadfastness
(left leg)

Security
(right leg)

7 Dialectica: The Art of Logic

The Virgin

At Apollo's request a woman now stepped forward whose countenance was somewhat pale due to the effort of thinking, but whose glance was acute and penetrating. Her eyes looked out with keen observation, and her long hair fell in layers, carefully dressed. Her clothing was a cloak from Athens.

In her hands she carried something that was unknown in ancient Greek schools. Her left hand held a snake, rolled into a ball. In her right hand she held a number of patterns, carefully engraved in wax and decorated in contrasting colors. The patterns are attached to the snake with a hook hidden under her cloak.

When someone wants to take hold of one of the patterns, the hook draws him to the snake and he is bitten by its sharp teeth. He is also seized by the coils and can be put into any desired position. When someone declines to take one of the patterns, Dialectica overwhelms him with questions, while the snake pops up and coils itself around the listener in such a way that he has to surrender to the will of his questioner.

Dialectica has a compact figure and a swarthy complexion. She says that she was raised in an Egyptian cave and moved to Attica in Greece, to

The Virgin Dialectica
with Aristotle

69

the school of Parmenides.[26] She had withdrawn there because stories were told that she had engaged in shameless behavior, but then she devoted herself to the greatness of Socrates and Plato. (after Martianus Capella)

Stature

According to Alanus, the Virgin Dialectica has a stature very different from those of Grammatica and Rhetorica. He also calls her the Virgin Logica. Alanus describes her as having a lean face, the cheekbones clearly visible. She has a harmonious figure. She is awake all night. Her hair hangs down tangled in "disputes"; no comb can straighten it out. Her eyes can compete with those of an eagle in fieriness. In her right hand she has a flower—a lily? In her left hand a threatening scorpion. One hand spreads honey, the other gall. The one rejoices in laughter, the other brings sorrow and tears—all the time the polarities of receiving and chasing away, striking and caressing, anointing and thrusting, loving and poisoning.

It is a Hegelian picture, with its theses and antitheses, that Dialectica evokes. Behind these world polarities stand the great creative forces from the astral world: sympathy and antipathy. But her robe holds to the middle; it is as a synthesis. It is gathered in the middle; it is not soiled but neither is it like a blinding light.

Dialectica fights for the true with a double-edged sword. She fashions the axle for the chariot of Prudentia, world intelligence, in which the latter has to make a journey through the heavenly realms.

Categories

The practice of dialectic liberates thinking from its body-bound prison. Dialectic is a practice on the basis and out of the categories of Aristotle. These categories relate to each other in a particular way akin to grammar. For this reason, the images of Grammatica and Dialectica stand very close to each other in Martianus Capella's imagery. Aristotle also builds up his categories out of the language. And it is the world word, the Logos, which becomes Logic. The ten categories of Aristotle are the following:

Substance	e.g., woman, horse
Quantity	e.g., two feet, three ounces
Quality	e.g., white, grammatical
Relation	e.g., double, half, larger
Where	e.g., in the town
When	e.g., yesterday, next year
Position	e.g., he stands, she sits
Having	e.g., he has courage
Doing	e.g., she cuts, he burns
Suffering	e.g., he is burned

These examples are taken from chapter four of Aristotle's book on the categories. Earlier he clearly showed that he had developed the categories out of the Logos, the Word. Every word that is spoken without a connection to something else indicates a substance, quantity, quality, relation, a where or when, or a position, having, doing or suffering. The ten categories have a certain relationship to the ten Sephirot, which are used by the Jews as a religious conceptual framework.

Dialectica works with the categories which she calls "terms." On the wax tablet that she carries in her right hand, figures appear all the time. They arise out of the movements of her thought, for instance, when two or more premises lead to a conclusion. An example: The human being speaks; Alexander is a human being; therefore Alexander speaks.

This is an example of a logical, dialectic form of thinking. Logic therefore generates movement of thought and is for this reason an eminently spiritual activity.

Thinking and intelligence

In human thinking, in our ideas, lives our guardian angel. In the Middle Ages, what was meant by "intelligence" was often the angel. If we would have asked a person in the Middle Ages for his intelligence, he would have turned around to see if we meant his guardian angel as his protective intelligence.

Thinking in images

In ideas the angels weave their images into the human soul. Thinking becomes imagination. This living thinking is also very important in our time, because the angels try to impart major and exceptional impulses to humanity in the form of images. These are impulses that would develop the human being in the direction of religious freedom, to a true picture of human threefoldness, and to brotherhood in which the suffering of fellow human beings is felt as our own.

Dialectica is able to transport us into this sphere of the angels. She brings us then into contact with our guardian angel who is, in the perspective of our individuality that has gone through many lives, the carrier of our destiny.

Dialectica feels related to ancient Greece. She is able to discern deceit. She was raised in Egypt, went to Greece, and has the great spirit of Socrates and Plato.

Perception and thinking

The Virgin Dialectica investigates the life forms of, for instance, animal, plant, rock and human being. Then she investigates the species: lions, tigers, cows or roses, cruciferous plants, herbs, et cetera, of which she considers the differences, characteristics and capacities. She formulates definitions, describes different properties in their wholeness, and can explain how different parts form a whole. She distinguishes different species or properties. She knows the different concepts that are evoked by the same word, such as Lion—the animal and the star sign—or a more general word such as clothing.

Dialectica contemplates the fundamental question of the subjective and the objective, which also lives in existential philosophy.

In all the descriptions, the space of left and right is clearly present; it is the space of thinking and discernment, and therefore uniquely human.

Cautious wisdom

Dialectica's virtue is cautious wisdom: Prudentia.

Aristotle as teacher

On the West Portal of Chartres Cathedral we see Aristotle sitting at the feet of the Virgin Dialectica.

Exercise
We study the following polar pairs within the ten categories of Aristotle:

Substance
(What is it?)

Quality   Quantity
(How is it?)   *(How much is it?)*

Having
(Which properties?)

Time   Space
(When was it?)   *(Where was it?)*

Position
(How is it placed?)

Suffering   Doing
(What is it undergoing?)   *(What is it doing?)*

Relation
(How does it relate to its surroundings?)

The left hand column—Quality, Time, Suffering—has a more receptive character and can therefore be said to be passive, while the right hand column—Quantity, Space, Doing—has a more giving character and can therefore be called active. The remaining four categories form the middle column between the receptive and active concepts. In these three ways we can describe something that has touched us.

In my experience it can be wonderfully inspiring to describe something—a tree, an animal or a concrete person—with the help of the ten questions that belong to the categories and are shown in italics. It should be something, or someone, we have actually observed at one time and that, or who, has made an impression on our memory.

Step 1: Choose a flower, animal, mineral or person.
Step 2: Describe the subject with the help of the ten questions.
Step 3: Try to condense the ten answers into a description, poem, drawing or painting.

Working with the ten categories of Aristotle in this manner brings reality to life and enriches our experience. The essence of the subject comes to life. Dialectica becomes an art that enlivens the wisdom of the world in us.

8 The Trivium as Practice of the Threefold Cross

The Trivium consists of the three subjects: grammar, rhetoric and dialectic. They are always led by the Virgin Grammatica whose subject is the first of the curriculum of the Seven Liberal Arts. The three Virgins Grammatica, Rhetorica and Dialectica are described and pictured as having specific spatial orientations.

Grammatica

The Virgin Grammatica is oriented to the space in front and behind the human being. She bestows her grammatical insights in the form of a lesson book that she holds in front of her when she is with her pupils, while she usually holds a cane behind her back. Her forward gesture is one of giving; she hides her force behind her. Her image is on the West Portal of Chartres Cathedral.

Rhetorica

The Virgin Rhetorica is sometimes described in her joy, sometimes in her wrath, in her mastery of tuba and horn. She lives in language. She speaks out of the horizontal plane, in which the arms move that she spreads out in speech, in support of a rich feeling life. Working in the horizontal plane she separates the upper from the lower.

This becomes most evident in Martianus Capella's description, where she appears with sword and shield. We may imagine that she beats on her shield with her sword with a horizontal gesture, and thus forcefully demands attention with the words "Listen, Friends!"

Dialectica

The last of the Virgins of the Trivium is Dialectica who works and battles in movements of thought in the encounter of left and right. On the left she has the scorpion and gall, on the right the flower and honey. In the picture she is holding a dragon and a torch. The torch illuminates thinking, the dragon manipulates. The space that splits the human being into left and right represents the faculty of discernment.

The threefold cross

In the practice of grammar, rhetoric and dialectic these spaces are formed and brought into equilibrium so that in the soul a threefold cross will grow. In the process of working with the Virgins of the Trivium, the connection with the archetypal image of the human being is established.

On the path of practicing grammar we conquer anew the upright posture of the human being; we position ourselves between restraint and force, directing our will toward a balanced position. This expresses the virtue of justice, the fruit of the practice of grammar. From standing up straight we stride forward, we walk a path of life formed in justice. As we have seen, it is the sphere of the Archai, the Spirits of Personality, which is related to this faculty.

In the exercise of dialectic, practitioners strive to enliven their thinking in such a way that the right connection with the Angel can be found. Here we are in the space where we become discerning human beings, and in which the right half of our body is separated from the left half. Here we reconquer thinking in its relationship with the archetypal image of the human being.

When we practice the art of rhetoric we strive to find the right relationship with the Archangel by moving through our exercises in the world of rhetorical speech. Speaking is an exercise for the middle realm of the human being. In rhetoric, we place ourselves in the horizontal plane of feelings, which separates the upper and the lower in the human being.

By experiencing and bringing to realization in grammar the life of the will, which separates front and back, by strengthening in dialectic the thinking that separates left from right, and by experiencing and reinforcing in rhetoric the life of feeling, we create connections with the three spatial orientations which have from time immemorial worked on the true human image as world thinking, world feeling and world will. In our time, it is up to the human being to seek in freedom a new connection with these creative world forces so that thinking, feeling and the will may be harmonized and brought into balance.

The way, the truth and the life

The three spatial orientations intersect on our sternum in the vicinity of the heart. This is eminently the place to experience the work of that Being who said of himself: "I am the Way, the Truth and the Life." Out of this point and from the activity of this Being, the Christ, the power of the Resurrection works in the *realm of the will* on the Way we walk, Light radiates into the *realm of thinking* with which we seek for Truth, and Love flows out of the *feeling realm* in which our speech becomes Life enhancing.

In the practice of the Trivium the archetypal image of the human being can come to realization out of the words "I am the Way, the Truth and the Life." And this can lead to the healing of tendencies toward one-sidedness that turn human beings into caricatures of their original archetypal image.

Parzival and the threefold cross

During the age of the Mysteries of the Round Table and the Mystery of Golgotha, a lofty individuality was withdrawn into higher worlds in order to bide his time waiting until the time was ripe for his special work. He remained away for centuries, and finally he came back as King Titurel, to whom the Holy Grail was entrusted, the cup that had been brought by angels from Golgotha to the West. During long ages of preparation, this great individuality worked from the spiritual world into Europe and its mystery centers.

In those times, many spiritual and secular leaders of humanity were inspired in this way, and we can understand their work only in this light. The saga of the Holy Grail relates that the cup with the collected blood of Golgotha was brought by angels to Europe. Titurel received this cup. He kept it hovering above the countries of Europe, and only after centuries did Titurel descend with it from spiritual heights to the earth to found the Mystery Center of the Holy Grail on the mountain of salvation (Montsalvat). He could do that only after several people were mature enough to receive the secret of the Grail. Everyone mature enough for this initiation was called Parzival. The story of one such Parzival shall be told.

A Parzival had purified his soul of all earthly wishes and selfishness through long meditations and concentration. He was a Cathar and stood pious and pure before his master Titurel, who told him that all the forces that Parzival had acquired through his long years of meditations and concentration were now to be used to bring forth his higher "I." He now stood objectively over and against himself.

First he had to sacrifice his intellect. As a result, as is written down in the esoteric script, he saw his physical being as a symbol. The entire physical world also disappeared for him. In its place he saw a great sprouting plant-tree as large as the entire earth. It was full of rising sap and in its top, a great white lily. He saw that the white lily grew out of the tree of life. Then he heard a voice behind him, the voice of Blanchflor, who said: "That is you!" And he knew that what he had gained by his meditations had formed the image of this lily. He saw in the lily his soul cleansed of passions and desires. The lily was magnificent, to be sure, and perfectly formed, but it was surrounded by an odiferous atmosphere that caused Parzival pain. He realized that this smell symbolized everything that he had set outside himself through catharsis and that this now surrounded him like an atmosphere. He learned that he must take all that back into himself, that he must transform this painful smell of the lily.

The image of the lily disappeared. It became dark around him. Another symbol arose out of the darkness for Parzival: a black cross entwined with red roses. The tree of life was transformed into the black wood of the cross with the sprouting, fragrant roses arising on it because of the absolute devotion of the lily to this tree. And Flor's voice spoke behind him: "Thus you should become." The smell of the lily had disappeared; the red roses had absorbed it. Parzival, however, saw that this purification was not enough, that he must nail his lower self on the black cross and conform to the life of Christ; he must take it into himself so that the red roses would blossom. He understood that the tree of life had been transformed into the dead wood of the cross, but also that because of this the lily would change into blossoming roses.

After these experiences Parzival went to a place of solitude, and let these symbols work within him day and night. With time, the symbols paled, yet the effects of their power remained. This power awakened a new experience. In the deep solitude in which he stood he looked around. He looked forward and backward, up and down, left and right. And he sensed the great unity in everything. He sensed that this unity envelops everything, like a great Enveloper. He experienced how the great Enveloper sent him forces from all sides, and he felt himself as a point, as the middle point, the center of these forces.

He then became conscious of two forces flowing through him. From the one side he felt a stream that pushed him to be dissolved entirely in the Godhead, in these forces of the Enveloper. But from the other side a force came that appeared to lead him into himself and appeared to give him a center. Thus he felt from one side a stream that flowed through him and strove toward complete dissolution in the Godhead, in the forces of the Enveloper; but from the other side came a power that wanted to take him by the hand and lead him to develop his own self. And while these two forces worked on him he felt a third power that joined together the previous two into an encircling movement, an enveloping space.

1. We have to learn to devote ourselves entirely to the first power, which works in us. It is the power we also apply, though unconsciously, when we concentrate on an object. In contemplation we must find this power.
2. The second power is needed to be entirely ourselves, to maintain our own self. We use this power in order to have enthusiasm, initiative for our life in the outer world.
3. The third power, which forms a circle around us, enables us to see all the joyful and sad experiences of life without absorbing them into ourselves.

In these experiences we recognize the power that works in the cosmos, that also works in the stars around us. This cosmic circle is usually drawn as the third straight line of a triangle. If we become acquainted with this power we can look upon what life brings us in joy and grief, with equanimity. We will know that everything comes into being from necessity, the driving law of karma.

Parzival had achieved these three powers; he devoted himself to them. Then, from the right and left, as supports under his arms, there came to him something like warm and cold wings. From the left he felt a supporting power, warmth and a spiritual fire, and on the right a power that was cool and made him stand firm. Then, in the region of the larynx, he experienced currents from both sides; they came from the angel of light who carried the spiritual light of wisdom to humans. He drew this spiritual light into himself. Then, in the silence, he heard sounds from the world of the harmony of the spheres. It was as if he received another two small wings in the region of his head, with which he could understand in the harmony of the spheres the purpose of the evolution of humanity and the world.

Again he tarried for a time; darkness enveloped him again. From above his head power streamed into him, and he experienced in this stream the power of the Father God, the creative power that enabled him to feel himself as a creation of this Creator. All these experiences grew together into one all-encompassing experience for Parzival. He felt his own being in the form of a pentagram. He knew himself as son of the Father. He saw the truth of the Rosicrucian verse:

> Ex Deo Nascimur
> *From the Father we are born*
> In Christo morimur
> *In Christ we die*
> Per Spiritum Sanctum reviviscimus.
> *Through the Holy Spirit we are brought to life.*

All of this Parzival experienced as he stood in solitude before Titurel.[27]

Three pre-Christian sacrifices

In Grammatica lives the memory of the first sacrifice of the archetypal Nathan soul in the age of Lemuria, when the senses were purified and the human being achieved the upright posture. Even now this uprightness is brought about in the child by the Christ working through a being from the ranks of the Archai. *Ex Deo nascimur.*

In Rhetorica we find the strength from the second sacrifice which took place in the age of Atlantis. It brought the polarity between metabolism and consciousness into equilibrium. In language, this equilibrium is introduced by the Archangels. *In Christo morimur.*

In Dialectica, the third sacrifice of the Nathan soul becomes accessible in the strengthening of thinking, feeling and the will, in the sphere of the Angels. *Per Spiritum Sanctum reviviscimus.*

Lucifer and Ahriman

Evil is a theme that humanity has had to deal with in all time periods and in all peoples. Rudolf Steiner described it as learning to handle extremes. Lucifer is the spirit of pride and Ahriman the spirit of hardening.

Bringing the three realms of the life of the will, the life of feeling and the life of thinking into proper relationship with each other creates balance in the soul life. In the space before and behind the will life, Lucifer reaches to the sternum and Ahriman to the back. Lucifer can come as far as the teeth, Ahriman to the cane.

In the space under and above, Lucifer reaches to the head, Ahriman to the limbs. Only in the space right and left do Lucifer from the left and Ahriman from the right reach each other; here they wage a battle.

9 The Quadrivium

World and Grail mystery

In the Quadrivium, the practitioner meets the world with the abilities he has newly acquired in completing the Trivium. Now he becomes an investigator of the kingdoms of nature and their mutual relationships. In the Trivium the practitioner finds a new equilibrium through which he can achieve a new connection with the world and the kingdoms of nature within the realm of the Quadrivium which follows.

In the Trivium a strengthening takes place of thinking, feeling and the will out of the world of the Trinity, by archai, archangels and angel beings. The transition from the Trivium to the Quadrivium is one from a focus on the human being as fulfillment of the true human image, to an exploration of nature. We are like Parzival who encountered the Grail mystery for the first time, and now goes back into the world with newly acquired capacities.

In the Quadrivium the practitioner, as "renewed" human being, finds his relationship and connection with the whole of the kingdoms of nature. He does this in a fourfold manner following a methodically composed plan.

Arithmetica and the mineral kingdom

In Arithmetica the connection with the mineral kingdom is explored. The arithmetical consciousness focuses, like a counter, on that which can be measured, weighed and expressed in numbers. The mineral realm is the preeminent example of the physically observable world. In the human constitution this corresponds with the physical body.

Geometria and the plant kingdom

Geometria widens the measurable world to one of active relationships of forces and powers. In the geometry of the cube, the sphere, of all platonic bodies, we find primeval images for the principles of form that underlie all life processes.

In modern projective geometry, the art of geometry is expanded and in its expressive power reaches even more directly into the formative world that underlies the life forces. In anthroposophical spiritual science, this is called the realm of the etheric forces or formative forces. The realm of formative forces finds in the outer world its preeminent expression in the plant kingdom. In geometry, and even more so in projective geometry, the world of plants can be understood and expressed in its active etheric forces. We also recognize these forces in the different forms of landscape.

Musica and the animal kingdom

Musica is oriented to a more hidden world; neither the eye nor the sense of movement are able to perceive the world of music, but only the ear. In the experience of tone and harmony, it is in the first instance the human soul that is addressed. Anthroposophical spiritual science calls this part of the human constitution, which is the carrier of the soul forces, the astral body.

The animal world produces sounds. Especially the birds, living in the element of the air, are the ones that create the sounds of music. Just as geometric forms, in their mobility, have their point of impact in the element of water, in fluidity, so music has this preeminently in the element of the air.

Astronomia and the human kingdom

Astronomy directs its attention to the starry world on the border of the observable world. It is manifested only in the form of dots. In Greek times it still called forth an imaginative consciousness that transcended physically observable things. In our time this imaginative consciousness needs to be developed in a new way through the human being's own activity. This will call into being a completely new relationship with the world of stars. The stars indicate the most unique aspect of the human being. The human "I" is akin to the stars, and out of anthroposophical spiritual science, we may surmise that each human "I" has one particular star with which it has a special connection. Astronomy makes the transition from the planets to the fixed stars. The zodiac is its particular expression.

A fourfold world image

In the Quadrivium we explore in the four disciplines—arithmetic, geometry, music and astronomy—the four elements of the world. This can lead us to an understanding of the creative worlds which underlie the human physical body, ether body or body of formative forces, astral body and "I." In this way the four human "instruments," the four elements of his constitution, are explored in the Quadrivium.

The investigation of the world, of the mineral, plant, animal and human kingdom by way of arithmetic, geometry, music and astronomy leads to the *human being*.

Just as the Trivium encompasses the Trinity and the archetypal image of humanity, in the Quadrivium we find the human being out of the kingdoms of nature in the fourfoldness of his instruments.

10 Arithmetica: The Art of Numbers

The Virgin

This Virgin, with her striking appearance, radiated from her forehead a beam of light that was nearly imperceptible. This beam split into two, then three and four until there were ten. The beams all came from her forehead and rayed out in combinations of two or three, but although their lines appeared to continue into the infinite, in due course they faded and came together again into a unity. [Think of the decimal system! – F.L.] A cloak that revealed the multiplicity of nature covered her intricate undergarment. The fingers of the Virgin moved at a speed that was imperceptible to the eye. (After Martianus Capella)

We greet Arithmetica as the first of the Virgins of the Quadrivium presented by Alanus ab Insulis. Even though she is the fourth among the Virgins, in her whole being and working she could be the first. Her delightful beauty, her sensitivity and loveliness are her strengths, but she also does not lack keen acumen.

Her face is like an open book in which the letters are messengers of her heart. With her intellect, modesty and clarity she vanquishes her sex through her masculine mind. She has a naturally rosy complexion

The Virgin Arithmetica with Boethius

and tolerates no makeup or paint. Her head is inclined toward the earth without becoming heavy. She considers the Pythagorean tables which she carries in one hand, while with the other hand she arranges numbers in columns; and she can also fight.

Her garment

Her garment, woven from fine, yellow flax, Byssos, envelops her limbs kindred to the stars. The delicacy of this dress is unsurpassed. Here speaks a stilled image; nature is vanquished by art in the language of the figures and the speech of the script. From her unity the multiplicity of numbers comes forth. With her cloak she teaches the great realm of arithmetic. As he does with all the Virgins of the Seven Liberal Arts, Alanus gives the cloak of Arithmetica a lot of attention. It expresses the essential being and capacities of the Virgin. Her teaching is written into the cloak.

Every human, every living being wears an invisible cloak right on the skin: it is the body of life forces. Here lies the origin of human knowledge that has become capacity.

Mercury

With Arithmetica we see that the cloak, in the meaning of its forms, speaks to the art of arithmetic. She organizes, she determines relationships in the world. Martianus Capella described her with similar powers, and for Mercury she was the most impressive among the seven Virgins. Martianus also described the lightning-quick movements of her fingers with which she counts and can even give number values to language by addressing the name of Zeus (*Arche*) in numbers (717).

Like Alanus, Martianus described the tenfold beam of light, the sacred ten of Pythagoras. Even the gods are impressed by the way the light beams appear on her forehead and how the many become one and one becomes many. Pythagoras, standing among philosophers, follows the Virgin. She speaks: "All gods come forth from me."

Sacred numbers

Number, the sacred monad, existed before all gods. She offers her services to Mercury. The monad is the Father of the all; it is Jupiter/Zeus.

Number 1: Arithmetica describes the nature of one in the world all. There is one God, one universe, one sun, one moon. Some call the monad friendship, others collaboration. Thus she continues, describing two, three and so on to ten. She reveals the quality of the number from the observable world. Martianus distinctly orients himself on observable reality.

Number 2: With two, Arithmetica describes polarities, such as good and evil.

Number 3: A perfect number. Father, mother, child.

Number 4: Four is the number of solid bodies.

Number 5: Five is directed to the universe with the five senses.

Number 6: Six is the number of natural relationships such as size, color, form, space, rest and movement. It is the number of Venus.

Number 7: The number of the octave: five whole and two half tones. She pauses at seven. The Greeks already knew the seven-year rhythm.

Arithmetica shines like the morning star, and no one will decline her offer to help Mercury. She connects herself to him in her freely chosen offer of service. This gives us insight into the relationships of the seven Virgins to the seven planetary forces or gods. These relationships are self-chosen collaborations of the soul forces of the human being with the macrocosmic planetary forces.

Number and quality

Arithmetica expresses herself in numbers: prime numbers, even and uneven numbers, rich and poor, cubic and flat numbers.

The number 6 is a perfect number because the sum of its quotients is equal to the original number:

$$6 : 6 = 1$$
$$6 : 3 = 2$$
$$\underline{6 : 2 = 3}$$
$$6$$

Similarly 8 is a poor number because the sum of its quotients is less than 8, whereas 12 is a rich number because the sum of its quotients is 16.

Arithmetica deals with all number relationships, such as:
Cubic numbers: 8 = 2 x 2 x 2 (length, width, height)
Flat numbers: 4 = 2 x 2 (length, width)
Prime numbers, which can only be divided by themselves; they are poor because of their restraint.

Temperance

The virtue that proceeds from the art of arithmetic is also the fruit of cooperation. It is the virtue of Mercury, temperance.

Boethius as teacher

In Chartres, Arithmetica is attended by Boethius, Roman statesman and philosopher who lived from c. 470 to 525 CE. He served Theodoric the Great and was the author of *The Consolation of Philosophy*.

Exercise 1
What is one in the world? Give your own answers, for example, one world, one love, and so forth. Do this with 2, 3, and so on to ten.

This is especially fun to do in a group because, in principle, every answer is right, provided it has a reason. In the first part of this book we saw already that Trevrezent also asked these questions of his pupil.

Exercise 2

Discover whether a number which plays some role in your life is poor, rich, perfect or prime. Write the number down together with all the numbers by which it can be divided. For instance:

$$8 : 2 = 4$$
$$8 : 4 = 2$$
$$8 : 8 = 1$$

Add the quotients, in this case $4 + 2 + 1 = 7$ which is smaller than 8; therefore, 8 is a poor number. The Virgin Arithmetica calls a number poor when it passes itself off as larger than what its quotients add up to. The number 12, for instance, is a rich number because the sum of its quotients is larger than 12. Perfect is a number when the sum of its quotients is equal to itself. And an example of a prime number is 7 because it can be only divided by itself, resulting in the quotient of 1.

This exercise changes our relationship to numbers. The numbers acquire their own particular signatures.

Exercise 3

Nicomachos, who continued the work of Pythagoras, discovered a way to find the series of perfect numbers. Take a series of numbers, for instance, 1, 2, 4, 8, 16, 32, 64, and so on. Add the first two and then add the next number to the result, continuing this through the series:

$1 + 2 = 3$ (a prime number)
$1 + 2 + 4 = 7$ (a prime number)
$1 + 2 + 4 + 8 = 15$ (not a prime but a poor number)

For those series for which the sum is a prime number, multiply the last number in the series with the sum. The product of this multiplication is a perfect number. Thus for the above example:

$2 \times 3 = 6$
$4 \times 7 = 28$
6 and 28 are indeed perfect numbers.

The perfect number indicates the ideal condition of the moral and, especially, the balanced individual. It preserves the right *measure* in the relationship between the outer world and one's own inner faculties.

Exercise 4

The Virgin Arithmetica also knows friendly numbers. These are numbers that mirror each other in the addition of their quotients. The first two friendly numbers are 220 and 284. We can divide 220 and the quotients will be 1, 2, 4, 5, 10, ... find all the quotients, add them up, and you will arrive at 284. Do the same thing with 284 and you will get 220.

At first sight, 220 appears to be less than 284. However, it is a rich number, while 284 appears to be more than 220, but is a poor number. In this way two friends can complement each other. By really living into this process when doing the exercise we can experience a moment of genuine, living truth.

It is not easy to find other such pairs of perfect friends, but they do exist. It is quite a task.

11 Geometria: The Art of Space

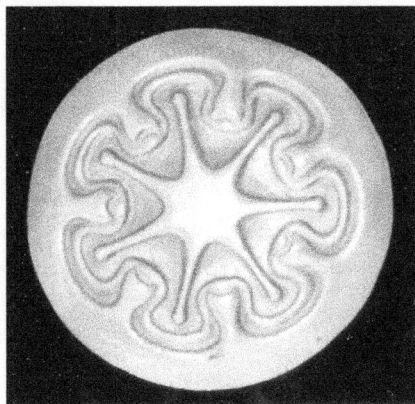

The Virgin

Before Geometria appears, Pallas Athena is honored as the *Hebdad*, the virginal seven. The Seven Liberal Arts as a whole are placed under the protection of Pallas Athena. She is the virginal goddess who was born from the head of Zeus. The owl of wisdom was consecrated to her, and she wears the head of Medusa on her breast. Before Geometria starts speaking she wipes a lock of hair from her face. Everyone who is engaged with geometry is used to speaking Greek. Geometria carries an abacus. (After Martianus Capella)

Pallas Athena

Pallas Athena overcomes the old clairvoyant consciousness that lived in the snake-wreathed head of Medusa. In this way she is, one could say, the heir of Perseus who, watching in the mirror of his shield, slew Medusa. Perseus practiced reflective thinking in order to overcome the old clairvoyant experience that lived in imaginations. Through the practice of the Seven Liberal Arts, however, Pallas Athena reestablishes the connection between intellectual thinking and cosmic intelligence, which since time immemorial has been protected by Michael.

Pallas Athena strives to preserve the connection between terrestrial science and cosmic intelligence. Science can then become art.

Geometry

Geometria appears as the fifth among the Virgins. With a long staff she points to the earth and indicates the sea, mountains, rivers and lands. She works with what is measurable on earth. Geometria lives with the earth in all its multiple forms. She encompasses the surfaces of lands, lakes and oceans. She can awaken a great love for our magnificent blue planet. Her name itself already indicates the earth (geo).

Alanus ab Insulis gives a better description of Geometria's outer appearance than Martianus Capella. In his description she inclines her face slightly, but without evoking a feeling of weakness. She gives her attention to that on which her spirit rests and which reveals itself to her soul.

She carries a staff or a twig with which she encircles the sphere of the world. Her garment is sprinkled with little dots of dust, but these do not obscure the quality of the garment. Also the form and design of the garment indicate her honor and beauty.

She teaches measurement—how to catch the infinite and enclose the finite. She practices the laws of triangle, square and circle. It is the etheric world which she uncovers, makes visible and explores through physical observation.

Earth and sciences

Geometria is also oriented to the earth as a whole. She explores earthly space both in connection with the cosmos and in its own inner connections. Just like every living being, the earth is also alive with formative forces. The congealed activity of these formative forces can be experienced anew in the geological constitution of the earth.

Geometria awakens our love for the form-language of the earth, and this gives hope in our time when the complaint of the earth can be so clearly experienced in earthquakes and other natural calamities.

Novalis, the poet from the time of German idealism in the 19th century, lived intensely with this art. Besides being a poet, he was a

The Virgin Geometria with Euclid

hardworking mine engineer with a great love for the secrets of the earth. He worked his knowledge of the earth into his novel—only a fragment—*The Disciples at Sais*.

This story describes a pupil in the mystery school of Sais who collects shells and stones. He arranges them in formal patterns and orderly rows. In the changing forms and variety of patterns a mysterious language begins to speak. It is the form language of nature which the pupil learns to read in this way. Thus he learns to know the earth and he loves her. He searches for a mysterious Virgin who carries all this life in her and imbues it with her spirit:

> How much longer I shall stay here I know not. It seems as though I should remain forever. ... She [the Virgin] is immanent. When I go about here in this belief everything induces a higher semblance, a new order, and all is directed toward One Goal. Each object then becomes to me so intimate, so dear, and what yet appears to me as curious and strange suddenly becomes like a household word.[28]

These words of Novalis are like a motto for the practice of the art of Geometria.

Formative forces and projective geometry

In geometry we enter in an artistic way the world of planes which, with its life forces and formative forces, underlies the physically observable world. In the minerals, for instance, we see in the crystal the moment of coagulation, and thus the moment when a particular effect of the formative forces is made visible and held in matter. It shows the formative forces that worked in the past and holds these fast.

In the plant kingdom we see how new planes are continuously appearing through the unceasing activity of the formative forces. The development of the plant occurs between the point and the plane. The seed is point, the cotyledons plane, the stem point, the petals plane, the stamen point and the pistil plane. And these are in constant arithmetical and geometrical movement.

This explains why Martianus described a strong connection between Geometria and Arithmetica. In their interaction we observe in an artistic manner the connection between the etheric world and the physical world. In our time geometry may be expanded to projective geometry.

Virtue

The virtue that is cultivated by Geometria is *hope*.

Euclid as teacher

In Chartres, Geometria is accompanied by Euclid, the father of geometry. He lived around 300 BCE in Alexandria.

Exercise 1

Imagine a circle that grows out of a point. We let the circle grow out of the point. In doing this we start with a point and then arrive at the circumference.

We can also do it the other way around: we start at the circumference and let the circle contract into the point.

This exercise brings about a breathing movement in our inner being, in which we connect ourselves with the world.

Exercise 2

- On a walk, collect stones that appeal to you.
- Put them in an orderly row by form, color or substance.
- Let the row be for a few days (outside or inside) and look at it a few times every day.
- After three days, make a drawing of the row from memory.
- It then becomes possible to draw the whole row as a gesture. The individual forms now turn into a stream of color and form.

Exercise 3

Draw a circle with a center. Draw another circle which in four or five places is pushed in from the outside, while out of the center forces work from the inside out.

Draw a third circle on the basis of the previous one showing how forces from inside and outside can work on each other.

This can result in a series of seven drawings of which the fourth or fifth show the most complex relationship between inner and outer and the next two or three become more simple again. The seven planetary seals that are shown at the beginning of the chapters describing the Seven Liberal Arts arose in this way on the basis of seven places on each circle where outer and inner forces work on each other.

This geometry exercise is quite refreshing and stimulates the inner health and clarity of our thinking.

12 Musica (Harmonia): The Art of Harmony

The Virgin

Harmonia (Musica) comes forward between Phoebus Apollo and Pallas Athena. She is of noble stature, and her head is covered with ornaments and glistening gold. Her cloak is adorned with thin platelets of gold that tinkle and twinkle at every step she makes and with every movement of her body. In her right hand she carries a shield on which many circles are drawn, woven together and continually changing in the most surprising figures. The different circles form moving and varying tones into a symphony. In her left hand she carries tiny, miniature instruments made of pure gold. (after Martianus Capella)

Orpheus

Alanus compares Musica with Orpheus, the Thracian seer who, with his song-softened stone, transformed forests, changed the course of the water in rivers and, most of all, was able to settle disagreements and tame the animals. The musician works especially on the astral body of the human being. A popular saying has it that angry people have no songs. Music, song harmonize the soul life.

The Virgin Musica with Pythagoras

99

Musica

Alanus describes how Musica shows living images in her garment that tell the story of peace. She seeks no battle, but shows in cheerful pictures what music can bring about in joy and peace.

She describes the intervals between the tones. In the interval we observe the harmonious relationship between two tones. At every stage of cultural history a particular interval played a key role in musical experience.

Human development

In late Lemurian and early Atlantean times, this key interval was the seventh. Later, and continuing into post-Atlantean times until the Middle Ages, it was the fifth. Then, in the late Middle Ages, it became the third, and here Musica indicates moods of joy and sadness in the major and minor third.

In the future the octave will grow in importance, but in our time it is still difficult to experience the octave. The soul first needs to go through a future development. The experience of the octave will be a symptom of a future step in the evolution of human consciousness.

Martianus Capella goes even further in his description of Musica. He says that she also discusses measure, rhythm and melody:
- melody as free movement,
- rhythm as the power that connects and carries the music, and
- measure as the principle of will which, however, may also cause rigidity.

Under rhythm, Musica discusses the ancient Greek rhythms: iamb, trochee, anapest and dactyl. In these four rhythms, the soul lives in the world. The four temperaments can be brought into balance by these rhythms.

World soul and Musica

Musica enables the practitioner to observe and explore the world soul in connection with his or her own soul.

Breath plays an important role in music, for the rhythm of the breath is related to the zodiac. On average, we breathe 25,920 times a day, that is 18 times a minute. The number 25,920 is the so-called Platonic year, the time in which the vernal equinox has completed the full circle of the zodiac. This number encompasses the entire starry world related to the sun as the center of our planetary system.

In one world day of 25,920 years, the planets and stars complete a mighty movement. This is also the case with the starry body (astral body) of the human being in one day. Musica is related to the world soul.

Virtue

The virtue cultivated by Musica is *charity*, love as a social good.

Pythagoras as teacher

In Chartres, Musica is accompanied by Pythagoras, the Greek philosopher who died around 500 BCE. He developed the doctrine of the orderly working of numbers and of the earthly rendering of the music of the spheres.

Exercise 1

With a group of people, form a circle and start, all at the same time, a self-chosen tone. Try to hold on to your tone in harmony with those of the others and listen to the sound pattern of all the tones together. Is it in harmony or is there dissonance? Try it again with a different tone.

The exercise enables us to live into the intervals in the social process of singing together. We experience the social aspect of music.

Exercise 2

Find something in nature that makes a sound. Transform it into an instrument. When this is done by several people together, it is possible to create an ensemble.

13 Astronomia: the Art of Reading the Stellar Script

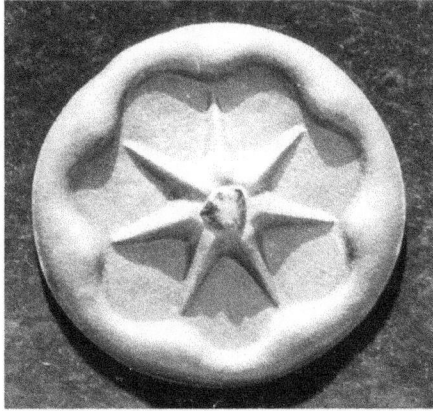

The Virgin

There appeared before the eyes of the spectators a hollow sphere of heavenly light, filled with a transparent fire that moved round and round, and enveloped the Virgin Astronomia. Several planetary beings, particularly those who influence the destiny of human beings, were taken up in this light. The mystery of their bodies and movements was revealed. Even the heavenly spheres radiated in this shining light. Even lower gods, etheric, terrestrial, sub-earthly and water beings became visible to the astonished onlookers.

Covered with beautifully cut polished and precious stones that adorned her cloak in magnificent patterns, Astronomia stepped out of the sphere of light. Her forehead was as the stars, and the locks of her hair sparkled. The feathers of her wings were as fine as crystal. When she moved through space, a golden mist hung in the air. In one hand she held a sextant and in the other a book with the computations of the periods of the orbits of the planets, their progress and their retrograde movements. The tables and drawings were executed in the colors of the various metals. The gods smiled to her and some of them adored her beauty. (after Martianus Capella)

The Virgin Astronomia
with Ptolemy

In his *Anticlaudianus*, Alanus ab Insulis points out that she always carries her head high so she can see the stars. As we have seen, her garment is covered with cut stones. Alanus says, with emphasis, that her garment glows with precious stones. The golden cloak itself is like the stars. She teaches the laws of the stars, the periods of their orbits, their appearing and disappearing. She teaches the heavenly realms, she describes the zodiac and the summer and winter constellations of the stars. She investigates the movements and relationships between the different planets. In all this she is precise and descriptive. With a keen eye she describes heavenly phenomena and their relation to the earth. Thus she teaches astronomy from observation, as this is also taught in the seventh grade of Waldorf schools.

Constellations and world views

Astronomia is the last of the virgins described in Alanus' *Anticlaudianus*. She directs her gaze to the periphery of the world, to those regions where the human soul and spirit being has its origin and from where it makes its appearance through birth on earth. In the zodiac the twelve world directions are named that bestow a signature on the individual striving of each human being, as it comes to expression in the way he or she thinks and stands in life. Rudolf Steiner distinguishes and explores these twelve world orientations in the lecture cycle *Human and Cosmic Thought*,[29] a rich source for anyone who wants to immerse himself in this subject.

The starry constellation of our birth is a picture of the end of our previous life. The constellation at death has a significant relationship to the constellation at birth in the next life. In this way the starry script communicates something concerning the individual biography to the extent that it has been completed and in that form has become a point of departure into the future. In the stars is written the name of the person who went through the portal of death, and who thereafter appears anew through the portal of birth.

In the early 20th century, anthroposophist Guenther Wachsmuth did a lot of research into this. He compared the horoscopes of a number of historical personalities on the basis of descriptions of two different lives of these people that Rudolf Steiner had given in his karma lectures. One of the most significant personalities described by Rudolf Steiner is John the Baptist. Steiner spoke of four different incarnations of this individuality: as the prophet Elijah, John the Baptist, the renaissance painter Raphael, and finally the poet in the era of German idealism, Novalis. Wachsmuth mapped the various birth and death horoscopes and arrived at a surprising picture relative to the positions of the various planets.[30]

The Cathedral in Chartres is dedicated not only to Mary but also to John the Baptist. The teachers there felt a very close relationship with this individuality. A magnificent statue depicting John the Baptist can be viewed on the North portal.

On the occasion of a celebration on his festival day, Alanus ab Insulis spoke the following words about John the Baptist: "John the Baptist was a voice, a voice that called. He is like a hero of the future, light of the light, the morning star that proclaims the rising of the sun."[31]

Schionatulander and the reading of the stellar script

In *Titurel*, a tale told by the Grail poet Wolfram von Eschenbach, we hear how Sigune, Parzival's aunt, together with the knight Schionatulander, encountered a dog that wore a collar with the stellar script of the signs of the zodiac. Sigune read in the collar's script how from every starry sign a virtue can be developed. The dog then ran away, and new destiny complications arose as a result of Schionatulander's chase of the dog. The name of the dog was *Garde vias*, which means "Mind your path." In the dog the stellar script appeared as a pointer for the life path of the individual.

In the same stellar script, Trevrezent, Sigune's brother who lived in solitude as a hermit and Grail messenger, read that Parzival had been called to the Grail. He read it in the mirror of the moon which, bearing sun powers, also reflects the stellar script. Through the sun and moon, the stars in the stellar scripts told the story of Parzival's life destiny. Here again we see an interplay of forces of the stellar script and the life destiny of an individual. Astronomia leads human beings into this sphere of their individual life destiny and thus also to the world from which the human "I" comes forth.

Virtue

Astronomia awakens the virtue of *faith*, the power of faith. When we have faith in someone or something, we can also be faithful. Faith is the foundation of the virtue of faithfulness.

Ptolemy as teacher

In Chartres, Astronomia is shown together with Ptolemy, an astronomer who lived around 150 CE in Alexandria. He placed the earth at the center of the universe.

Exercise
- Draw a circle.
- Divide the circle into twelve equal parts.
- Draw in each part, in the correct sequence, the symbol of a constellation of the zodiac.
- Write the names of friends, relatives or family members in the part of the zodiac in which their birthdays fall.
- Notice conspicuous clusters of names in certain constellations, and other places where there are no names at all.
- Consider the whole as a self-created firmament of family and/or friends. Of course, we can do this also for the colleagues with whom we work, or for clubs or associations with which we are connected.

It is fun to do this exercise. It is like a calendar that shows all our destiny companions against the background of the stellar script.

PART 3
INSIGHT INTO THE MYSTERY

14 The Seven Liberal Arts as Modern Grail Exercise

Mary Magdalene and the mystery of the Holy Grail

In Wolfram von Eschenbach's tale of Parzival, we find the symbolism of the wandering knight in search of the Holy Grail. A few years ago the theme of the Grail took center stage again due in part to Dan Brown's book, *The Da Vinci Code*. In this adventure story, the Grail mystery is identified with the person of Mary Magdalene. Rudolf Steiner once described Mary Magdalene as carrying the sentient soul of Christ. What did Rudolf Steiner mean by this?

The sentient soul is that aspect of the soul life of the human being that strongly lives in the impressions it receives through the senses. This faculty of the soul was developed during the Egyptian cultural epoch. The ancient Egyptians lived in the world as this appeared to their senses in all its forms and colors. Witness of this are the magnificent multicolored and gold objects of art they left behind from their ancient civilization.

It is remarkable that, in the Gospel of St. John, Mary Magdalene is the first to meet the risen Christ in the early morning of Easter. St. John described this in the following words:

> Early on the first day of the week, while it was still dark, Mary Magdalene went to the tomb and saw that the stone had been removed from the entrance. ... Mary stood outside the tomb crying. As she wept, she bent over to look into the tomb and saw two angels in white, seated where Jesus' body had been, one at the head and the other at the feet. They asked her, "Woman, why are you crying?"
>
> "They have taken my Lord away," she said, "and I don't know where they have put him." At this, she turned around and saw Jesus standing there, but she did not realize that it was Jesus.
>
> "Woman," he said, "why are you crying? Who is it you are looking for?"

Thinking he was the gardener, she said, "Sir, if you have carried him away, tell me where you have put him, and I will get him."

Jesus said to her, "Mary."

She turned toward him and cried out in Aramaic, "Rabboni!" (which means *teacher*).

Jesus said: "Do not touch me, for I have not yet returned to the Father. Go instead to my brothers and tell them, 'I am returning to my Father and your Father, to my God and your God.'"

Mary Magdalene went to the disciples with the news, "I have seen the Lord!" And she told them that he had said these things to her.[32]

Mary Magdalene sees Christ as the gardener, the caretaker of the life forces in the world of plants, bushes and trees. She is often represented as surrounded by budding plant life in spring and gazing at the being of Christ, so familiar to her, in the midst of the ever-industrious life forces in burgeoning nature.

In the scriptures found in Nag Hammadi in the 1940s, the close connection between Christ and Mary Magdalene is mentioned. The *Gospel of Mary* [Magdalene] contains a description of Andrew's and Peter's indignation with this special relationship:

When Mary had said this, she fell silent, since the Savior had spoken to her about all these things. But Andrew answered, saying to the brothers, "Say what you think about what she said. I do not believe that the Savior said this. These teachings are of strange ideas."

Peter also opposed her about all this. He asked the others about the Savior, "Did he really speak to a woman secretly, without our knowledge, and not openly? Are we to turn and all listen to her? Did he prefer her to us?"

Then Mary wept and said to Peter, "My brother, Peter, what do you think? Do you think I concocted this in my heart or I am lying about the Savior?"

Levi answered, saying to Peter, "Peter, you are always angry. Now I see you contending against this woman as if against an adversary. If the Savior made her worthy, who are you to reject her? Surely the

Savior knows her very well. That is why he loved her more than us. We should be ashamed and put on the perfect person and be with him as he commanded us, and we should preach the Gospel, without making any rule or law other than what the Savior said."[33]

Mary Magdalene was very close to Christ, and therefore she experienced him in living nature on Easter morning. Peter attacked her. The name Peter means "rock." He worked out of the power of rock, which indicates the forces of the physical body. Peter approached the world from external facts while Mary Magdalene, out of the realm of the sentient soul, perceived the forces of the etheric world.

In the Middle Ages, the life forces of Christ were experienced in the symbol of the Holy Grail. The Grail is the vessel in which the blood of Christ was preserved after the crucifixion on Good Friday. This blood bestows new life on the world and humanity, so said the various Grail stories. Parzival was called to guard these new life forces.

After endless wanderings Parzival entered the Grail Castle and saw a woman who carried the Grail into the great hall. This lady, who had the name of Repanse de Schoye, carried the Grail vessel on a cloth of green silk. She was the guardian of the true Grail secret, which is connected with the new life forces that have been flowing into the earth since the death and resurrection of Christ. In many respects this carrier of the Grail resembles Mary Magdalene within the circle of the apostles. Just like her predecessor in the time of Christ, she has an intimate relationship with the Christ mystery. In this sense we can see Mary Magdalene in connection with the Grail, but not in a physical sense, as suggested in *The Da Vinci Code*.

On Easter morning, Mary Magdalene met the risen Christ in the garden. She lived with living nature and beheld, with the power of the sentient soul of Christ, that the earth atmosphere was filled with new life. She also saw his radiating being that caused these new life forces to flow into the earth, and therefore she thought at first that he was the gardener.

It is said that Christ cast out seven demons from Mary Magdalene. Because of this she has always been the archetypal image of the human being who bears the Seven Liberal Arts in herself as virtues.

The Seven Liberal Arts form a path that enables us to become familiar with the planetary forces through exercises and with the way these forces are controlled by planetary intelligences.

Kundry and Parzival

Parzival was proclaimed Grail King when he had achieved the ability to bring these seven forces into balance in himself. Kundry, the messenger of the Grail, showed him the way. In Richard Wagner's opera *Parsifal*, Kundry had been Herodias in a prior life, the person who had caused the beheading of John the Baptist. Wagner let Kundry say this literally in the opera. Rudolf Steiner also recognized Kundry as the same individuality as Herodias. Kundry carried her destiny as Herodias with her in her etheric body. And this etheric body was purified the moment when Parzival was found worthy to be called to become Grail King.

The seven chakras and the Seven Liberal Arts

The Seven Liberal Arts as a path of exercises work into our habits and, therefore, into our life body. The life body has seven power centers that are related to the chakras or lotus flowers. The practice of the Seven Liberal Arts is therefore also a path to develop the lotus flowers.

We can now make the following overview:

Astronomia	Saturn	Memory
	Crown chakra	*8-petalled lotus flower*
Geometria	Jupiter	Thinking
	Third eye	*2-petalled lotus flower*
Rhetorica	Mars	Speech
	Larynx	*16-petalled lotus flower*
Grammatica	Sun	Protection
	Heart	*12-petalled lotus flower*
Musica	Venus	Power of love
	Solar plexus	*10-petalled lotus flower*
Arithmetica	Mercury	Connection
	Limbs	*6-petalled lotus flower*
Dialectica	Moon	Life, imagination
	Procreation	*4-petalled lotus flower*

Herodias

Herodias represents for Parzival the unpurified life forces. She makes use of magic in a dark, obscure way. In the sense of *Anticlaudianus*, she is under the influence of Alecto; in the Grail story this is equivalent to being part of the realm of the black magician Klingsor.

Modern human beings have the freedom to choose in what way they wish to develop their supersensible organs, the lotus flowers. The liberal arts continue to be a path of spiritual exercises to develop the lotus flowers in a harmonious way. And thus they open the possibility to develop spiritual consciousness in a healthy and moral manner.

The way to the Grail proceeds in seven stages, which Rudolf Steiner described in his book *An Outline of Esoteric Science*. He even called the content of this book the science of the Grail.

The seven planets are part of our constitution in the form of the seven lotus flowers. Parzival was a pioneer who went through a conscious development of the lotus flowers, beginning with the head and going down from there.

Alanus ab Insulis and the Grail

The way Parzival traveled was continued by Alanus ab Insulis. In his time in the town of Vezelay (France), there stood a magnificent cathedral dedicated to Mary. Alanus traveled through all of France and sojourned for a long time at the court in Montpellier.

As we have already seen, he knew the secrets of the two and the seven. The seven indicates the Seven Liberal Arts, but also the development of the seven lotus flowers as the spiritual organs that can bestow on human beings a harmonious connection with the spiritual world. This is the path of the practice of the Seven Liberal Arts. Alanus called the human being who traveled this path in the right way a knight.

The archetypal image of such a knight is Parzival, and Alanus continued his work. It is the Grail mystery that connected them with the Virgins of the Grail, who are at the same time the Virgins of the Seven Liberal Arts.

15 The Seven Liberal Arts and the Primeval Teachers

The habits a child develops in its life are formed by an ensouled education. Each of the seven Virgins can be active in the soul of the teacher and that of the pupil. These seven soul forces develop into capacities as they are absorbed into the flow of the life body.

Rhythmical repetition

This occurs by the rhythmical repetition of the curriculum as this is applied by the seven Virgins. These seven sisters are, as it were, soul beings that work on the education of the life body. The life body then becomes the carrier of new capacities.

The formation, through exercises, of life habits, which then manifest as life skills, is brought about by the active soul forces of the teacher. A good relationship between pupil and teacher is of great importance in this respect.

Freedom

Freedom is an essential element in the development of the modern human being. In order to accompany young people in the right way in our time, one has to be able to keep a distance and, at the same time, accompany the pupil in his or her own learning process. To the extent human beings develop the impulse of freedom more and more, they will also grow in their ability to think and perceive on their own.

Primeval teachers

Hinduism speaks of the primeval teachers of humanity. The wisdom that was inspired by these primeval teachers was written down in the Vedas, the sacred books of the Hindus. These primeval teachers did not appear in physical form but worked through inspiration from the spiritual world.

Rudolf Steiner described how these primeval teachers gradually refrained more and more from working directly into human beings because they respect human freedom.

Moon stronghold

They sought a spiritual dwelling place in the vicinity of the earth and found this in the sphere of the moon. The hard surface of the moon can be experienced as the wall of their stronghold. This castle of the moon is a name that speaks to human imagination, just as the Grail castle dominated the stories and poems of Europe for centuries.

Karma

The life of the human being, child and adult, is filled with adventures and vicissitudes. In the view of the ancient Indians, these events were viewed in the light of the concept of karma. Also in Rudolf Steiner's view, karma is an essential element in human life. After death the human being goes through a "review" of life, just as people who had a near-death experience have reported.

In this review the primeval teachers help us learn from our life by intensifying the images that arise then. (In some training situations, video recordings are used that enable students to witness their own actions. Most instructive!)

Rudolf Steiner sometimes called these primeval teachers the book-keepers of karma. They watch over the learning moments after death as the basis for the development of new learning situations in a subsequent life.

Retrospect in seven aspects

The primeval teachers direct their attention to the different spiritual impulses of the human being. They distinguish seven of these, and they are connected with the different planets, just like the Seven Liberal Arts. In the summary of this sevenfold retrospect of the past life lies the seed of the destiny of the subsequent life.

The following qualities are formed into an overall picture in relation to the moving heavenly bodies, to be metamorphosed into capacities in the next life. This table shows how the primeval teachers accompany, one could say escort, the human being between death and a new birth, and how this is an archetypal image for everyone who accompanies pupils through learning processes and wants to transform these into new skills and capacities.

Moon	Prudentia	*(cautious judgment)*	Constructive ability
Mercury	Temperantia	*(temperance, moderation)*	Movement
Venus	Charitas	*(love, charity)*	Love, beauty
Sun	Justitia	*(justice)*	Protection
Mars	Fortitudo	*(courage)*	Speech
Jupiter	Spes	*(hope)*	Wisdom, overview
Saturn	Fides	*(faith)*	Inner soul warmth

The teachers of Chartres and the primeval teachers

In the Middle Ages this knowledge was preserved in the School of Chartres, where there was still a secret awareness of karma and reincarnation. The inspiring presence of this age-old Indian knowledge of the primeval teachers lived in the exercise of the Seven Liberal Arts as practiced in the friendly contact between teacher and pupil in Chartres.

The Heavenly Virgin

We find this knowledge of the seven hidden primeval teachers also in a Christian image: the Heavenly Virgin in the Apocalypse of St. John. She stands on the moon and has the seven moving stars in her hand. From this image the teachers of the Seven Liberal Arts derived their inspiration. For the teachers in Chartres, the image was also connected with the inspiration of the primeval teachers from the mysterious stronghold in the sphere of the moon.

16 The Seven Liberal Arts and the Life between Death and Rebirth

When human beings go through the portal of death and lay aside their physical bodies, their life bodies expand into a world of images that show their entire completed lives like a panorama. Subsequently, their spiritual core moves through the seven planetary spheres like an arc that spans the time between death and a new birth.

The Moon Sphere and Dialectica

In beholding the panorama and, in the Moon sphere, reviewing and judging these images—when the etheric body has also been laid aside and we live through our past life again in reverse order—we are helped by our dialectic capacities to penetrate this world of images in thought. Gradually, the human being becomes wise and prudent, with the result that our spiritual core receives the virtue of dialectic (Prudentia) upon our return to the earth.

Mercury and Arithmetica

In the sphere of Mercury, we review the moral and immoral aspects of our previous life. If we practiced arithmetic on earth, it has become an art, and appropriate relationships will have grown with people around us. When the soul descends to earth again it will, in the Mercury sphere, the sphere of the spirits of community, the archangels, receive respect and honesty in right relationships (Temperantia).

Venus and Musica

Then follows the sphere of Venus. During our life on earth, the Virgin Musica helps us prepare a right relationship to this sphere. Musica lets us experience harmony and awakens our best feelings. It is no accident that singing and music form an indispensible part of religious cults and rituals. In the Venus sphere we form a connection with the great questions of humanity as these are experienced in all world religions. The Archai bring these questions to us. When we have reviewed and worked with them in the right way in the Venus sphere, by the time we descend to earth again, the virtue of charity (Charitas) can be bestowed on us.

The Sun Sphere and Grammatica

Next, our soul-spiritual being reaches the Sun sphere. Here the human individuality works in community in the midst of many other individualities who work on each other's destiny and place this in the seed of the bodily constitution. This asks for justice (Justitia), and the practice of Grammatica forms the path of development of this virtue.

Mars and Rhetorica

In the world of Mars, the soul-spiritual being enters the sphere of the creative world word. Rhetorica prepares our connection with this sphere and can become the virtue of courage (Fortitudo) when the soul-spiritual being passes through this sphere again on its descent to the coming new life.

Jupiter and Geometria

In the Jupiter sphere, world thoughts are weaving. They live there as world perspectives, just as they can be experienced in geometry. The Virgin Geometria bestows the strength on our soul-spiritual core to experience this sphere consciously, so that we can receive the virtue of hope (Spes) when we descend into a new birth.

Saturn and Astronomia

Finally, Astronomia leads the soul-spiritual being to the midnight hour and to its awakening in its own individual aspect in relation to human and world destiny. This enables the soul-spirit on its way to a new earth life to remain faithful (Fides) to its own unique tasks and perceptions in relation to the destiny of humanity and the world. Astronomia enables us to experience Saturn consciously.

Sophia

Thus the seven Virgins support the human soul on its journey between death and a new birth. During life on earth, the practice of the Seven Liberal Arts prepares our connection with the seven Virgins. The result of this is that the soul garment for the succeeding life can be formed into a body of virtue in which the wisdom being Sophia can become human, *Anthropos*.

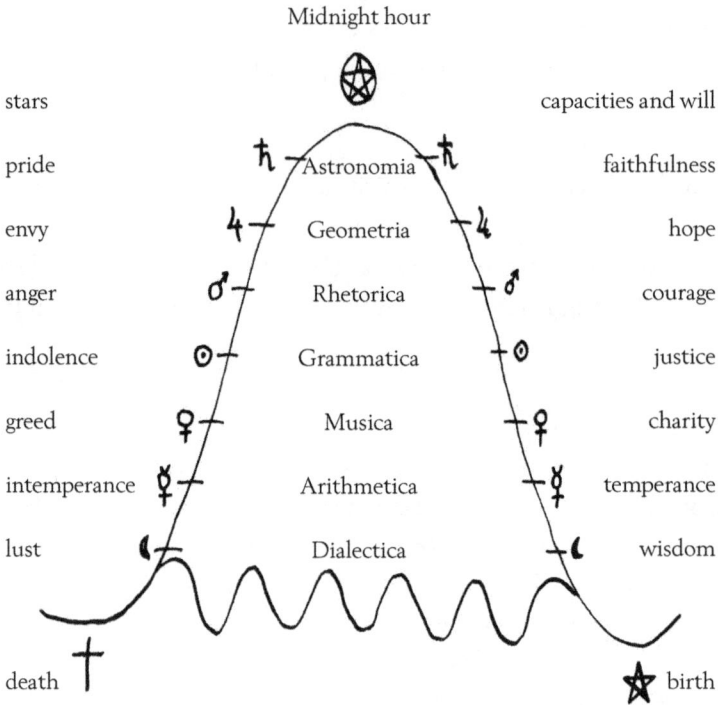

Midnight hour

stars		capacities and will
pride	♄ Astronomia ♄	faithfulness
envy	♃ Geometria ♃	hope
anger	♂ Rhetorica ♂	courage
indolence	☉ Grammatica ☉	justice
greed	♀ Musica ♀	charity
intemperance	☿ Arithmetica ☿	temperance
lust	☾ Dialectica ☾	wisdom
death †		✦ birth

17 The Seven Liberal Arts in Connection with the Planets

World view

In the world view of the Middle Ages, the earth was the center of the cosmos, and above it rose the planetary spheres, which are the homes and workplaces of the higher, hierarchically ordered spiritual beings. In this respect, consciousness in the Middle Age shows similarities with modern anthroposophy.

The planetary spheres

Anthroposophy describes the journey of the human being through the planetary spheres between death and rebirth. As we have seen, the soul passes through the spheres of the Moon, Mercury, Venus, Sun, Mars, Jupiter and Saturn respectively, and after midnight makes the journey in reverse sequence on the way to its new birth on earth.

The dynamics of this journey shows a striking resemblance with that of Prudentia in the chariot of the Seven Liberal Arts, as described in chapter 4. We may therefore expect each of the Seven Liberal Arts to have a special connection with one of the planets.

Dialectica can certainly be connected with the Moon sphere, Grammatica with the Sun sphere and Astronomia with the Saturn sphere. Arithmetica has an obvious connection with Mercury, and Musica with Venus. That leaves Rhetorica and Geometria. In the Mars sphere, we take the power of the word into ourselves, and Geometria can illumine the wide relationships of the realm of Jupiter.[34] This leads to the following picture:

Astronomia	–	Saturn
Geometria	–	Jupiter
Rhetorica	–	Mars
Grammatica	–	Sun

Musica	–	Venus
Arithmetica	–	Mercury
Dialectica	–	Moon

New capacities

Rudolf Steiner described that, when after the midnight hour we begin our descent to the earth and a new birth, we take in the power of memory in the Saturn sphere. Astronomia shows us the memory of the cosmos; she carries world memory in her being.

In the Jupiter sphere we take in the ability to think in broad concepts and connections. Geometria teaches us this and awakens this capacity. The Jupiter beings always help us in difficult issues and problems. Geometria carries world thought in her being.

In the Mars sphere, the human being absorbs the faculty of speech. Rhetorica evokes this capacity; she carries the world word in her being.

In the Sun sphere, the totality of an individual's strengths and weaknesses, talents and predispositions is formed in the right relationships to each other. Grammatica expresses this.

In the Venus sphere, world love becomes parental love. Here Musica awakens the experience of harmonious interrelationships.

In the Mercury sphere, Arithmetica enables us to find the right relationships to the earth and its peoples.

In the Moon sphere, Dialectica gives us the right life of imagination so that we can find our proper place in life, even down into the realm of passion and desire.

We can now complete the above table as follows:

Astronomia	–	Saturn	–	Memory
Geometria	–	Jupiter	–	Thinking
Rhetorica	–	Mars	–	Speech
Grammatica	–	Sun	–	Protection
Musica	–	Venus	–	Love
Arithmetica	–	Mercury	–	Connetion
Dialectica	–	Moon	–	Imagination

In these seven "steps" between death and a new birth, the entire threefold human being is built up as a spiritual archetype. The seven Virgins "reawaken" these archetypal capacities so as to create for us the soul forces for the next earthly life.

Virtues and vices

This shows us the connection between the planetary spheres and the Seven Liberal Arts. But now we have to make another step. Every planetary sphere has associated with it a specific virtue and a specific vice. The vice reveals itself in two ways, as Aristotle already pointed out. There is, of course, a relationship between the virtue and the vice. Relative to the virtue, the vice always shows up as too much or too little. In relation to the Seven Liberal Arts, this looks as follows (the virtue is preceded and followed by the two aspects of the relative vice):

Astronomia	unbelief	faith	gullibility	Saturn
Geometria	hopelessness	hope	rashness	Jupiter
Rhetorica	cowardice	courage	recklessness	Mars
Grammatica	indolence	justice	tyranny	Sun
Musica	greed	charity	lust	Venus
Arithmetica	excessiveness	temperance	self-deprivation	Mercury
Dialectica	dullness	prudence	pedantry	Moon

The Seven Liberal Arts were almost always taught in the sequence of the sun, moon and planets as these are reflected in the names of the days of the week:

Grammatica	Sun	Sunday
Dialectica	Moon	Monday
Rhetorica	Mars	Tuesday (Mardi)
Arithmetica	Mercury	Wednesday (Mercredi)
Geometria	Jupiter	Thursday (Jeudi)
Musica	Venus	Friday (Vendredi)
Astronomia	Saturn	Saturday

The curriculum of the Seven Liberal Arts has a relationship to the cosmic wisdom that lives in the sequence of the sun, moon and planets in the course of the week.

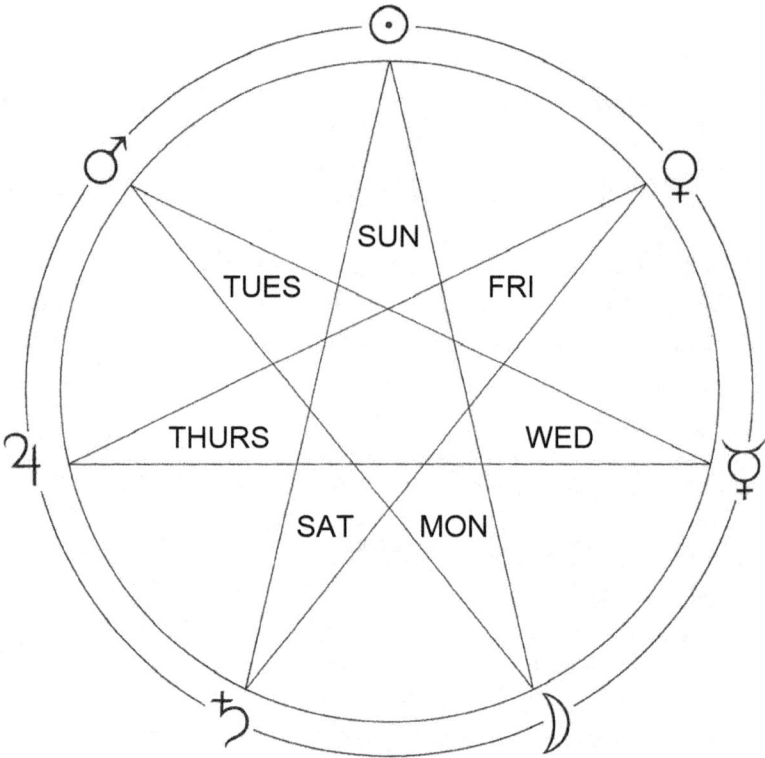

The sequence of the days of the week starts at the top with Sunday, then down on the right to Monday, and so forth in a seven-pointed star that indicates the sequence of the planets.

18 The Seven Liberal Arts and the Hierarchies

The spiritual hierarchies

In his book on the spiritual hierarchies, Dionysius the Areopagite was the first to present an orderly picture of the entire hierarchical structure of the spiritual world. He distinguished three times three hierarchies:

Third hierarchy:
    Angeloi (Angels)   Intelligences
    Archangeloi (Archangels)   Folk- and Language Spirits
    Archai   Spirits of Personality

Second hierarchy:
    Exusiai   Spirits of Form
    Dynameis   Spirits of Movement
    Kyriotetes   Spirits of Wisdom

First hierarchy:
    Thrones   Spirits of Will
    Cherubim   Spirits of Harmony
    Seraphim   Spirits of Love

The names in the second column were given by Rudolf Steiner. He used both names of each hierarchy in his descriptions of the human being and the world in his book *An Outline of Esoteric Science* (CW 13).

The Trivium

As we have seen, by the practice of Grammatica, Rhetorica and Dialectica, human beings develop three basic abilities, which place them again in the threefold cross of space. In the experience of the structure of language, Grammatica places us in the will, the space before and behind out of which we move walking into the world. Rhetorica places us in horizontal space of feeling in which we live when we speak. And Dialectica teaches us to make distinctions with the help of thinking, the space that separates left from right.

In thinking, which we practice in dialectic, we find our connection with the Angel that in the Middle Ages was called Intelligence. In speaking with feeling as practiced in rhetoric we find our connection with the Archangel, the Spirit of Language. In working with the will in structures, which we practice in grammar, we find our connection with the Archai, the Spirits of Personality.

In the practice of the Trivium, thinking, feeling and the will are strengthened and brought into relation with the beings of the third hierarchy.

The Quadrivium

In his book, *An Outline of Esoteric Science*, Rudolf Steiner gave an extensive description of the development of the earth and discussed four great phases in the evolution of the earth.

The first evolutionary phase took place in the element of warmth and he called *Old Saturn*. The second phase took place in a gaseous condition which he called *Old Sun*. The third phase passed into a liquid state and was called *Old Moon*. The fourth evolutionary phase, called *Earth*, is currently taking place in a condition of solid matter.

The Quadrivium brings human beings into connection with, and especially makes them conscious of, the beings of the second and third hierarchies which bestowed on them their fourfold constitution during the phases of Old Saturn, Old Sun, Old Moon and Earth. In the beginning of the Old Saturn evolutionary phase, the Thrones gave us the substance of warmth, which formed the basis for the physical body (the Archai, Grammatica, went through their "human" phase on Old Saturn). In the Old Sun phase, the Kyriotetes gave the life forces (the Archangels then went through their "human" phase, Rhetorica). On Old Moon, the Dynameis let their wisdom-filled powers stream into the human astral body (the Angels then passed through their "human" phase, Dialectica).

And in the beginning of the Earth phase of evolution, the Exusiai bestowed the "I" substance onto the human being as the basis of the "I" organization. Now human beings themselves are passing through the human phase, that of freedom.

After the Seven Liberal Arts have been practiced, the connection with Divine Sophia, who took a central position in Chartres Cathedral, becomes possible. She is surrounded by the beings of the highest hierarchies, the Cherubim and the Seraphim.

19 The Seven Liberal Arts and Intelligence

Cosmic intelligence

The guardians of the cosmic intelligence were conceived in all cultures as seven beings. Zarathustra called them the seven Amshaspands, and in Christianity we hear of the seven gifts of the Holy Spirit.

For a long time it was unusual in Europe to speak of seven intelligences that accompany and inspire humanity in its development. Now and then we find this knowledge in forgotten writings or poems. Rudolf Steiner revived this hidden knowledge and named the seven guardians of cosmic intelligence in all clarity and openness. He used the names which Abbot Trithem von Sponheim used in his book on the seven heavenly intelligences. The illustration to the right is of the original title page of this book.

In the picture, we see a group of gods and goddesses who represent the planets and the sun and moon. In the clouds above them are some small figures of angels who have the names of the seven intelligences. The following names are related to the planets, sun and moon:

Michael	–	Sun
Anael	–	Venus
Raphael	–	Mercury
Gabriel	–	Moon
Oriphiel	–	Saturn
Zachariel	–	Jupiter
Samael	–	Mars

Trithem von Sponheim described these seven heavenly beings as the mediators of cosmic intelligence and therefore also of the spiritual guidance of human evolution. Michael, as the sun being, is the principal one. Rudolf Steiner took this picture and went further, describing

126

Trithem von Sponheim, *On World History and the Seven Intelligences* (1532). Pictured are the seven planetary gods with their Latin names under their feet, and above them, the corresponding seven planetary intelligences as angels, carrying banners with their names.

the problems and challenges we face in order to think through, and experience, the points of view of these seven aspects of cosmic intelligence in our own personal intelligence.

The practice of the Seven Liberal Arts gives us the potential to pass through the qualities of the seven planets and thus learn to change points of view in our own development. This knowledge lived also in the School of Chartres, and for this reason Rudolf Steiner spoke in the framework of this sevenfold cosmic intelligence with so much enthusiasm about the School of Chartres, and the broad and remarkable way in which teachers such as Alanus ab Insulis and Bernardus Silvestris worked.

In the School of Chartres, the inspiring Virgins of the Seven Liberal Arts were experienced in all reality during the teaching process. Their presence at the artistic exercises in the different subjects was taken very seriously. These Virgins created a relationship with the seven guardians of cosmic intelligence, and for that reason, in the original plan, Chartres Cathedral was to have had seven towers as an image for the totality of cosmic intelligence.

The Virgins and the seven guardians of cosmic intelligences related to each other as follows:

Grammatica   –   Michael
Dialectica   –   Gabriel
Rhetorica   –   Samael
Arithmetica   –   Raphael
Geometria   –   Zachariel
Musica   –   Anael
Astronomia   –   Oriphiel

In the view of the teachers in Chartres as in that of Rudolf Steiner, they represent the whole of cosmic intelligence.

The development of personal intelligence

The practice of the Seven Liberal Arts has also facilitated the growth of personal human intelligence. It opens the possibility to experience the forces that work from the various hierarchies and also as our own personal forces in our thinking, feeling and will. The Quadrivium is oriented to the observable world and the processing of sense impressions, while the Trivium leads us into the world of thought and to the conditions required for the act of thinking.

Arithmetica is directed to the realm of counting and weighing: the forms that were created by the Spirits of Form, the Exusiai. Geometria brings these observations into movement, and thus lays the seed for mobile thinking. For instance, when we follow the process of metamorphosis of a plant from leaf to leaf, flower and seed in inner pictures, we live in imaginations. These are carried and woven with the forces of the Dynameis in the center of the head, around the place of the pineal gland where the crown chakra is located, and about which Rudolf Steiner spoke as the "Grail Castle in the brain."

Musica brings observations even deeper into the human organism. Here they are transformed into sensation, feeling, which can be perceived in the back of the head as inspiration bestowed on us by the Kyriotetes. And finally, Astronomia brings our perceptions into relationship with the creative powers of the Thrones.

When Parzival was proclaimed Grail King, all the beings of the seven planets were called on as the guardians of cosmic intelligence. In the time of Wolfram von Eschenbach, this could only be done in Arabic because, except for Michael, Gabriel and Raphael, uttering the names of the heavenly intelligences had been forbidden ever since the arrival of Boniface in medieval Europe (seventh century CE).

Parzival becomes Grail King when Kundry, the messenger of the Grail, evokes the seven planetary intelligences, because Parzival has achieved connections with all of them. Then he is able to find his way to the Grail again. This is not just an outer, but also an inner path which is connected with a newly developed personal intelligence, and with the hidden, as yet undeveloped powers in the brain that are concentrated around the pineal gland. The anthroposophical physician Margarete Bockholt described the way of Parzival in relation to the human head as follows:

> This part of the brain [the pineal gland] may well appear to us like a solid fortress with walls and moats, connected in all directions with the outside world, but at the same time also with the inner world of the human being. For we find under the "four hills," close together on the bottom of the fourth chamber in the brain, all the centers of the twelve nerves, which flow in from the entire organism into this one spot. ...
>
> The Grail has always had great significance in world history. From the Grail human beings received their most precious nourishment, the impulses that awakened their most noble side, and called on them

to collaborate in the development of the world. The Grail Legend is the story that places our souls before an important point in world evolution. We know much about this turning point from the lectures Rudolf Steiner gave, especially in the last years of his life. Through him we know that, before the Mystery of Golgotha, the wisdom that reigns in the world, and that is connected with the sun, was not experienced by human beings as something that belonged to them, but was administered as cosmic intelligence by Michael.

Then Christ, the Sun Spirit, descended to the earth and, in the succeeding centuries, the Sun intelligence descended with Him, so that in this way it came within reach of human beings and had to be adopted by them. This was the turning point when heavenly wisdom changed into earthly dullness, dumbness as pictured in the Grail Legend.

Then followed a time when humanity was shut out of the heavenly light. In earthly thinking, human beings had to transform the wisdom that had flowed down from heaven into their own thinking. Now however, we live again in a Michael era, and we are asked to bring, out of ourselves, the Sun intelligence we have transformed into our own thinking back under the dominion of Michael. This will open the possibility for human thinking to encompass world thinking. This is the Michaelic thinking we must conquer.

We can accomplish this by lifting our thinking out of the passivity in which it usually takes its course, and where it amounts to no more than a string of images called into being by outer observations. A type of thinking needs to arise that takes hold of thoughts out of our inner being, from our "I." In this connection, the pineal gland is of extraordinary significance.[35]

These forces can only be brought to their real development the moment that Parzival becomes able to take the point of view of another person. In the spirit of the Seven Liberal Arts, we now know that Parzival, at the moment when he was proclaimed Grail King, had the ability to take seven points of view, and therefore was qualified to represent for humanity the spiritual guidance that is exercised by the seven planetary intelligences. Rudolf Steiner said this in a very simple but distinct manner:

> Parzival must raise his interest above that of a mere innocent spectator to understand inwardly the commonality of all human beings, humanity's right, the gift of the Holy Spirit.[36]

Like Rudolf Steiner, Trithem von Sponheim said that the era of Michael would begin in the year 1879. According to both men, the seven planetary intelligences follow on each other in periods of around 350 years. The era of Michael was preceded by that of Gabriel, and before Gabriel, in the days of Alanus ab Insulis and the School of Chartres, Raphael was the time spirit. In the picture of the seven planetary intelligences, we see that Michael is placed with the sun which, as king, leads the line of the planets. In Chartres this was experienced in the same way because one always began the path of artistic practice of the Seven Liberal Arts with Grammatica, the sun art.

20 The Seven Liberal Arts and the Future

This book was written out of the realization that it is possible in our time to revive the impulse of Chartres. But this requires that we develop new forms of teaching and learning.

In our time it has become possible to speak about karma and reincarnation in an unprejudiced, open-minded way. For Alanus ab Insulis and the other great teachers in Chartres, this was still a living concept, and in working with their pupils they tried to keep it in mind. They did that in inconspicuous ways and were inspired by the mystery of the Grail.

Today many people are searching for a renewal of this impulse. I have tried to describe the Seven Liberal Arts in relation to the Grail mystery. In this connection my daily work as a school teacher is a never-ending source of inspiration. Teachers and pupils have continuous opportunities to go through a learning process creatively and autonomously, in the spirit in which it was done in Chartres.

In education we are constantly faced with measures that are imposed by the government. But it is the teachers together with the pupils who determine the learning atmosphere of a school.

In the Seven Liberal Arts as they were taught in Chartres, I have found a source from which I have been able to give my task in education a broad perspective that can reach far beyond just the transfer of knowledge. There is nothing airy-fairy or mystical about education in the sign of the Grail; on the contrary, it gives courage and enthusiasm to blaze new trails in education and explore new forms of learning. In my view this is a new, vital impulse for a form of education worthy of a human being.

It finds its example in the way pupils and teachers interact with each other. The teaching that the hermit Trevrezent gave to his Grail knights was inspired by the activity of the seven planetary spheres. This inspiration came to new life in the teaching of the Seven Liberal Arts as these were taught in the School of Chartres.

In this form of education, Alanus ab Insulis was able to bring his spiritual message. But his work went beyond that. Rudolf Steiner spoke extensively about Alanus in his karma lectures, and described his renewed activity right now in the early 21st century: His works continue in service of the renewal of the Grail mystery. The Grail mystery needs people in our time who are able to approach the world in a spiritual way without becoming strangers to the world.

A sevenfold path of learning is waiting for us to recognize it. Rudolf Steiner tried to make a contribution to this with anthroposophy. But he also pointed out that a true culmination of new spirituality would not take place until the early 21st century, and that the individuality of Alanus ab Insulis would play a central role in this.

What is needed now is a renewal of the mysteries. Rudolf Steiner called anthroposophy the science of the Grail.

Alanus will work in the spirit of Parzival and in order to do this he needs the opportunity to develop his capacities to the fullest.[37] A form of education worthy of the human being is the key to this, a form of education that will be a further development of what was laid as a seed in the Waldorf School impulse and is now asking for further development.

In this sense, this book is more than a general reflection on the Seven Liberal Arts. It is also a call for further renewal in education in service of young people, who bring capacities with them that have the potential of opening up completely new possibilities for dealing with the enormous problems humanity is facing at this time in its evolution. A form of education in seven phases can be a basis for this, because it has a direct relationship with human dignity in body, soul and spirit.

To strengthen human dignity, Rudolf Steiner gave the meditation of the Rose Cross. The black cross with the seven red roses around its center is like the human being who, instead of dead knowledge, develops living concepts on the basis of an artistic learning process through seven phases. The red roses blooming on the cross are then like the new sevenfold inspirational force of the human being who makes an original and creative contribution to the development of humanity and the world.

Endnotes

1   D.J. van Bemmelen, *Zarathustra, profeet van Christus*, Zeist, 1968.
2   Rudolf Steiner, *Turning Points in Spiritual History*, CW 60, March 9, 1911, SteinerBooks 2007.
3   *Corpus Hermeticum III*, tr. G.R.S. Mead (gnosis.org/library/grs-mead/TGH-v2/th207.html).
4   Iamblichus, *Theurgia or On the Mysteries of Egypt (De Mysteriis)*, ed. Clarke, Dillon, Hershbell, Atlanta, 2003.
5   In the Apocalypse of St. John, the Virgin is described as "a woman with the moon under her feet, clothed in the sun, and on her head a crown of twelve stars" (Rev. 12:1).
6   *Martianus Capella and the Seven Liberal Arts*, Volume II, *The Marriage of Philology and Mercury*, tr. W.H. Stahl & R. Johnson, Columbia University Press, New York, 1977.
7   Charles de Coster, *De legende en heldhaftige en roemrijke daden van Uilenspiegel en lamme goedzak in Vlaanderen en elders*, Amsterdam 1941.
8   Wolfram von Eschenbach, *Parzival, A Romance of the Middle Ages*, tr. Mustard & Passage, New York, 1961, verse 782; the next quotation is from verse 773.
9   Basilius Valentinus, *Von der Meisterschaft der sieben Planeten in Chemischen Schriften*, Erster Teil, Hildesheim, 1976.
10 Rudolf Steiner, *Theosophy*, CW 9, Anthroposophic Press, New York, 1994.
11 Op. cit., von Eschenbach.
12 Walter Johannes Stein, *The Ninth Century*, Temple Lodge 1991.
13 Walter Johannes Stein, *The Death of Merlin*, Floris Books 2008, Chapter 16: *The Seven Liberal Arts and the Twelve Philosophies*.
14 This view is confirmed in the book *Reise nach Byzanz* by Johanna von Keyserlingk, Basel, 1991, p. 173 ff: "Rudolf Steiner called Alanus ab Insulis 'the towering teacher' and he spoke of 'the tremendous images that flowed from his mouth like silver words.' He then described that Alanus was the leader of the heavenly council where the grand objectives of Michael were prepared ... He was a holy, primal teacher who brought his wisdom to earth in the course of time. He taught his pupils with silver magic words. Mighty is Alanus ... He is the same as Mani."

Johanna von Keyserlingk was careful in her words, but it is clear that she viewed Alanus and Mani as one and the same individuality. In Rudolf Steiner's view, Mani was born again as the historical Parzival. (See also Bernard Lievegoed: *Battle for the Soul*, Hawthorn Press, 1994.)

15   Notes by Elisabeth Vreede on Rudolf Steiner's esoteric lesson of August 27, 1909, Elisabeth Vreede Archive.

16   From Alanus ab Insulis, *Der Anticlaudianus Ode von der himmlischen Erschaffung des neuen Menschen*, tr. W. Rath, Stuttgart 1983, summaries made by F.L., tr. P.M.

17   Chretien de Troyes' *Perceval* was written around 1180 and Wolfram von Eschenbach's *Parzival* around 1200.

18   Op. cit., von Eschenbach, verse 121.

19   Chretien de Troyes, *Parsifal, the Story of the Grail*.

20   Op. cit., von Eschenbach, verses 235–236.

21   Pictured in the chapters describing the Seven Liberal Arts are the seven planetary seals designed by Rudolf Steiner. They were executed in different metals:

> Grammatica: Sun seal in gold
> Rhetorica: Mars seal in iron
> Dialectica: Moon seal in silver
> Arithmetica: Mercury seal in mercury alloy
> Geometria: Jupiter seal in tin
> Musica: Venus seal in copper
> Astronomia: Saturn seal in lead
> Several of the seals have a precious stone in the center.

22   Plato, *Timaeus,* Penguin Classics.

23   Alanus ab Insulis, *Der Anticlaudianus Ode von der himmlischen Erschaffung des neuen Menschen*, tr. W. Rath, Stuttgart, 1983.

24   Ibid.

25   Rudolf Steiner, *Guidance in Esoteric Training*, CW 42/245, Anthroposophic Press, 1994.

26   Parmenides was a Greek philosopher who lived around 500 BCE.

27   See Rudolf Steiner, *Esoteric Lessons 1904–1909*, CW 266/1, SteinerBooks 2007, August 27, 1909, Records, A, B and C.

28   Novalis, *The Disciples at Sais and Other Fragments*, tr. Una Birch, Classic Reprint Series, 2012.

29   Rudolf Steiner, *Human and Cosmic Thought*, CW 151, Rudolf Steiner Press, n.d.

30 Guenther Wachsmuth, *Kosmische Aspekten von Geburt und Tod*, Dornach, 1974.

31 Alanus ab Insulis, *Predigten zum Jahreslauf*, Stuttgart 1998, tr. P.M.

32 Gospel of St. John, 20:1 and 11 – 18, New International Version.

33 W. Barnstone & M. Meyer (editors), *The Gospel of Mary* in *The Gnostic Bible*, Shambhala, 2003.

34 Compared with the lecture of W.J. Stein quoted in chapter 2, Geometria and Rhetorica have here been switched. That Geometria can be connected with Jupiter is confirmed by Victor Stracke, *Das Geistgebäude der Rosenkreuzer*, Dornach, 1993.

35 Margarete Bockholt, *The Grail Castle in the Brain*, in Graalschrift no. 2, Summer 1987, Leiden.

36 Rudolf Steiner, *The Effects of Esoteric Development*, CW 145, March 26, 1913, Anthroposophic Press, 1997.

37 See Bernard Lievegoed, *The Battle for the Soul*, Hawthorn Press 1994, endnote 36 quoting Ehrenfried Pfeiffer: "Rudolf Steiner has said that Mani/Parzival could not yet find a suitable body, that all the forces he would be able to bring to an incarnation would be destroyed by modern education. ... By karma, Mani's incarnation would be due by the end of the [20th] century."

www.ingramcontent.com/pod-product-compliance
Lightning Source LLC
Chambersburg PA
CBHW020204090426
42734CB00008B/940